This House Was Full of People

MARY WALLACE KIRK

Locust

Hill

THE UNIVERSITY OF ALABAMA PRESS
University, Alabama

2nd printing. 1976

*Copyright © 1975 by
The University of Alabama Press
ISBN 0–8173–5314–3
Library of Congress Catalog Card Number 74–15395
All rights reserved
Manufactured in the United States of America*

Contents

Publisher's Preface

I first met Mary Wallace Kirk when she brought her manuscript, photographs, and etchings to my office. As is usual with a publisher, I looked at the Table of Contents, read a few pages, then looked at the photographs and etchings. I fell in love with all of them, and later my love was shared by all who worked on the book.

Locust Hill is the "biography" of an ante-bellum mansion, told through the lives of the family that flourished in it—a narrative told by the last of the line to inhabit Locust Hill.

Mary Wallace Kirk's artistry is unobtrusive; it is delightful, unique, and whimsically charming. Her nostalgia is not verbose or sentimental but filled with humor and the laughter of a childhood joyfully remembered. At the same time, it is firmly grounded in an awareness of inevitable transition, as beauty fades or is perhaps transformed.

With art both verbal and visual, Miss Kirk expresses through her words her love and respect for her family and through her etchings, interspersed among her anecdotes, her love and respect for the underprivileged people around her.

Locust Hill is a jewel, an heirloom—a tender portrait of a way of life whose last leaves are falling, but one that has been realized superbly well in the house where Mary Wallace Kirk still lives.

MLW

Sunset on the Tennessee   Mary Wallace Kirk

To my mother and father,

whose love and understanding

made my childhood

a very happy one

The places that we have roots in, and the flavor of their light and sound and feel when things are right in those places, are the wellsprings of our serenity. There must be something in them as important to us as a home slope is for a Douglas fir, an importance a geneticist has in mind when he says, "Plant local seed stock." Alienation does not come easily to living things, even in migration they contemplate a return. Granted, the affinity for the milestone places in a man's life is an affinity that is largely unstudied and this is not the place for extensive delving; we simply know that nostalgia has a purpose.

DAVID R. BROWER

Locust Hill

Introduction

I LIVE IN SUCH A HOUSE AS HARRY ASHMORE IN HIS *Epitaph for Dixie* says "is destined to become a gentleman's club, a boarding house, or a mortuary if it is not razed to make way for a supermarket"; a supermarket has already made a bid for some of the property, but it was declined. More than one hundred years of occupancy by the same family seems worth recording in this mobile age.

T. S. Eliot says that "home is where we start from." With some of us it is where we remain, where the roots of the spirit have their abiding place. There is something deeply satisfying about a house in which generations have been born and have lived together in small things—"where they eat the same dish; their drink is the same and their proverbs." At Locust Hill there has been no sweeping away of the old nor any indiscriminate adoption of the new, but the antique and the modern meet and mingle in happy relationship. From continuity one inherits a sense of security and a foundation for peace of heart that care cannot disturb nor sorrow take away. In the home of my people I not only feel the footsteps of their lives in mine, but I can hold happily to the values of the past that are fine and by an adoption of the best of the new attempt to build a more excellent present.

A few years ago when the late Lawrence Critchell visited Locust Hill he remarked after his first tour of the house, "This is a place where people have been happy." Later that evening as we sat on the porch after the other dinner guests had gone, he said, "These old Southern houses have long interested me, but this is the first time I have ever been in one. I have passed them and wondered what life was like inside. I had expected to find a Truman Capote atmosphere, but tonight the conversation has been as modern as a bull session at college." Recently a Birmingham seamstress came to renew the summer slip covers. One day after I had left her alone for several hours she said, "This house seems full of people—I don't mean ghosts. Even with you away I had no feeling of being alone. Something seems always to be happening."

Locust Hill is essentially a place for living. Though now I am alone in it, the tide of life still flows strongly, for its source is deep. So it is with houses that have been lived in continuously by the same family over generations. The rooms become impregnated with their presence. Did not Rilke say that houses and things are vessels in which those who came before us found and stored humanity and that in this fast moving world we today may be the last to know them?

I have had access to my mother's papers that tell of her youth and mine. And there are fragments of conversations and incidents in a journal that I was always going to keep in detail but never did. Because reminiscences were often a part of family talk, it is difficult to know how much I remember on my own and how much I remember from hearing it told. To have had a grandfather who had seen Peggy O'Neill and remembered hearing his father tell of experiences on the way to the Battle of New Orleans is to reach back in time with a possessive hand and bring forth things new and things old, things true and things circumstantial.

As a very little girl in a big house I associated almost exclusively with older people—my grandfather, my uncles, my father, and my mother. I unconsciously absorbed from them stories, customs, habits, ways of seeing and of remembering. Their interests were my interests.

In these recollections I have written of the familiar things of everyday in the way of life I happened to know as a child, convinced that its like will not come again.

House and Grounds

IN 1865 MY GREAT-GRANDFATHER, CAPTAIN JOHN TAYLOR
Rather, bought Locust Hill in Tuscumbia, Alabama, for three
thousand dollars in gold. This was after his plantation home in
Morgan County, Alabama, had been burned by federal troops.
Part of this money had been buried during the war, and part had
been carried by his daughter-in-law (who later became my
grandmother) and her maid in stockings sewed to belts under
their hoop skirts.

On a cold December day of that year the family moved in.
There were ten of them: my great-grandfather, his son, General
John D. Rather, and his wife, Letitia Pearsall Rather (my grand-
parents, whom I called Papá and Mamá, accenting the second
syllables), and their six children. As these children appear frequently in this story, I name them here. Three were by a former
marriage: George, Silas, and Eldon. George and Silas had just
returned from service in the Confederate army. The three
younger children were Hal, Ella, and Anne. Ella would later
become my mother. With them also as an important member of
the family was Sarah, my grandmother's maid, who became the
"mammy" of the younger children and was called Ghee.

The house was without steps or blinds; it had been whitewashed inside; on its floor were many bloodstains. Colonel
Florence Cornym had requisitioned it as his headquarters when
he occupied Tuscumbia, and later it had been used as a hospital
for wounded Confederate soldiers. During Reconstruction years

the old way of life was gone, property confiscated, desolation and defeat on every side. A price was on my grandfather's head. My grandmother's first purchase after moving into the house was heavy red material for curtains, which were drawn every evening before dusk lest he be shot through a window. The custom of drawing shades or curtains still lingers at Locust Hill.

JOHN TAYLOR RATHER, AGE NINETY-FOUR

Locust Hill was built in 1823 by Colonel William Winter. Age has given it dignity and character, but he gave it its fine proportions, great chimneys, handmade-brick walls thirteen inches thick, windows with deep reveals and charming wood-work. Rooms twenty feet square, their lovely mantels hand carved by a local wood carver, open off a central downstairs hall that extends from front to back, while the stairway, following a pattern set by Thomas Jefferson, is suppressed between two walls. Shut off by doors at the bottom, one opening into the hall and the other into the library, this stairway had advantages in heating as well as privacy. To a child it was a delight and truly "somewhere else instead." Wrapped in a red shawl, I loved to play there. It became my refuge when at six years I longed to be an author and write beautiful books for children.

Set back among trees with a sweeping lawn, Locust Hill has permanence and peace. It is beautiful in the way a well-loved face is beautiful. One approaches the house by a long box-bordered brick walk and on moonlit summer nights sees walls and chimneys towering ghost white among the trees. The moon-light makes a frosted filigree of the porch as crispy delicate as Venetian lace—a porch capacious in its passage across the front of the house and down one side; the scene of much family living. My grandmother planted the old English boxwoods down the front walk and Madonna lilies and roses on either side. The box-wood cuttings came from her oldest sister's home, Boxwood, where she first met my grandfather. The locust trees that were here in 1865 have long since died, but each year in April the numerous descendants with their creamy white blossoms lend beauty and fragrance to the grounds. There are many cherry laurels of the old variety, seedlings from the original one. The same is true of the boxelder, the prolific mulberries, and the paulownia trees. My grandfather planted the maples, mimosas, magnolia, the great oak that dominates one part of the lawn, and the four cedars, tall and majestic, across the front of the place. Two of them have been blown down in recent years, and

THE REAR GARDEN

the others have suffered "wounds and sore defeat" from glaze storms, but they valiantly wave floating plumes. To cut them down would leave a much "too lonesome place against the sky." On either side of the wide front steps were mounds and among their rocks were ferns and verbena; there were also fan-shaped frames with coral honeysuckle after the fashion of the time.

The flower garden at the rear of the house was my grandmother's special care. From her girlhood home, Locust Lodge, on the old Pond Creek Plantation, she brought the sweet Betsys, syringars, euonymus, Japanese quince (I loved to make leis of their bright red blossoms), spireas, periwinkle, altheas, daffodils, pink and blue hyacinths, iris, and flowering almond. All but the sweet Betsys are still here in more or less profusion. The flowering almond was a great favorite with my grandfather. I can remember how every spring he would cut with his penknife the first spray of blossoms and formally present it to my mother. It was my proud accomplishment to walk by the garden borders and call each of my grandmother's roses by name—Malmaison, Lamark, Microphylla, Safrano, Red Odeheat, Pink Daily, Giant of Battles, General Jacqueminot, Yellow Harrison, William Allen Richardson, Gloire Dijon, Bon Silene, Pearl of the Garden, Solfetaire, and Madame Joseph Schwartz. My best bloomers today are some of those time-proven varieties that by long conditioning have become inured to excessive cold and severe drought. Whenever I gather a bunch of Madame Joseph Schwartz's pale, pink-tinted, and chiffon-textured blossoms I never fail to recall those lovely lines of Ausonius:

> Did dawn come first or roses,
> Or did the Cyprian stain them from one shell?

At the end of one border was the "Hal" apple tree, so named because my Uncle Hal came in one afternoon from a horseback ride and, finding his mother among her roses, stuck his riding crop, a freshly cut switch from an apple tree, into the ground to have it grow into an exceedingly tall tree. I remember its good little russet-spotted apples.

My grandfather's special province was the vegetable garden. Beyond the flower garden and extending to the end of the block, it was noted for its great variety and abundance. There were tomatoes, lettuce, radishes, celery, potatoes (sweet and Irish), squash, eggplant, cucumbers, cabbage, and a patch of corn—a wonderful place to catch June bugs. You tied a long thread to one leg, ran with it, and so made the bug "June." The turnip patch was green winter and summer, and the Negroes were allowed to pick as many "greens" as they wanted, while at any time children raided the perennial shallot bed. There were sage bushes and parsley and an abundance of mint for ice tea and juleps. Beets, peas (the sweet wrinkled kind), beans (bush and climbing), and butter beans were there in succession.

ENTRANCE TO THE LIBRARY

Asparagus and strawberry beds, red and black raspberries, salsify, figs, peaches, apples, pears, and cherries, together with nectarines, plums, apricots, and horse apples—all were in the garden. Salsify was a great favorite among the vegetables because it was edible during the winter months, and no Christmas dinner was complete without its being served with turkey, rice, oysters, country ham, beaten biscuits, ambrosia, and cake.

As I sit here by the south window in the library, the favorite seat of my grandmother—after her death, of my grandfather; later, of my mother, and now mine—I can see the upstairs window of an old house, the one by which my grandmother sat to have her ears pierced for earrings when she boarded there and was a student at the Tuscumbia Female Seminary. Everyday she passed this house and looked up at the long line of locust trees across the lawn that gave the place its name, little dreaming that one day she would live here. Doubtless, she had to summon all

MARY WALLACE KIRK SITTING IN THE CHAIR BY THE
SOUTH WINDOW OF THE LIBRARY

her courage and humor to face that cold December day and the
barren, denuded house.

The view from this window has changed much since my
grandmother's time; trees and flowers have died and been replaced, but in the distance the line of low hills is the same, cloud

shadowed at noon or purple against the sunset sky; and each spring the same wisteria hangs its purple clusters over the window, its warm honeyed fragrance mingling with the scent of locust blooms.

Once screams came through this window when my grandmother looked up from her sewing to see a maddened bull crash through the white picket fence that surrounded the place and charge towards her little boy playing on the lawn. He was rescued, but with a fractured skull. There was no time to wait for the horse-and-buggy doctor, who was on a country call; so my grandmother put into place the fractured pieces and sewed over them with her needle and thread. When Doctor Desprez arrived, he said he would make no change, she had done his job so well. Her little boy recovered. Sitting here by this window listening to the tick of my great-grandfather's clock, as spring once more touches with tenderness the outside world, I am conscious not only of this intense moment, isolated, with all that it holds of the security and comfort of home, but of other moments—whole lifetimes, if you will—of those who came before, "those immortal, mild, proud shadows" who for more than a century have given Locust Hill its character.

> Who shall compute our harvest, who shall bar
> Us from the former years, the long departed?
> What have we learned from living since we started
> Except to find in others what we are?

Colonial Cottage

THE ONLY OTHER HOUSE ON THE BLOCK WITH LOCUST HILL
was a colonial cottage across the garden facing the street on the
north side of the block. There my mother and father lived for
the first few years of their married life, and there I was born.
The cottage is a story and a half. It then had dormer windows
and a gabled portico flanked by tree box. There was a lovely
garden, a scuppernong arbor, a summerhouse, and a flower-
bordered walk leading to it from the back porch. There was a
flowering crab apple tree as tall as the house. In the spring its
myriad clusters of pink-tinted, roselike blossoms made an exqui-
site mammoth bouquet. My mother often teased my father by
saying, "I married you to get this tree!" In this house were my
first recollections.

I remember a pair of red shoes. They must have been on a
table for I recall the flicker of firelight upon them. I remember a
special feeling when I had them on, and red shoes have always
symbolized for me a kind of light-hearted gaiety. I see my
mother in a dark red "tea gown" with a blue silk front and my
father coming home in the evening and playing with me, and
my nurse rocking me to sleep with that plaintive song:

> Oh, let's go down the Jordan
> Meet me at the river side,
> Oh, let's go down the Jordan
> Cross dry shod.

Preaching here, preaching there,
Preaching everywhere I go, my Lord.
Oh, let's go down the Jordan
Cross dry shod.

Morning after morning I stood by a low window looking
out over the garden and demanded that a certain poem be read
to me. I do not remember its title, only the sparkle of sunlight
on green leaves, tall white lilies, and the last line: "Good morning,
beautiful world." I sat in my little red chair at a small table
set up on the back porch for a late breakfast. The long porch
extended across the back of the house, then continued at right
angles to connect with the pantry and the kitchen, which was
two steps up. I ate something out of a bowl with a green border
and flowers painted in its bottom, and there was a little bunch of
flowers on the table. I remember picking violets, and I have been
told that one morning I came in with what I called a "bunch-
kay" of them and announced that I wanted to write some
"potry." My mother got pencil and paper, and I dictated the odd
line: "The sun is rising on the set."

One long summer afternoon I was playing with my doll in
the upstairs room where my mother was taking her afternoon
nap. On waking, she put on a white muslin "wrapper," the kind
that Southern ladies of that day wore over their gowns, and
proposed a tea party. I think she always felt a special obligation
to give companionship to her only child. To my great delight but
agonizing fear, she quickly leaned far out of the window and
gathered a handful of little yellow "sugar pears" from a tree
within reach. That was the same window where later, along with
old Mrs. Slipper-Slopper, I first caught a glimpse of "Mr. Fox"
carrying off the "gray goose" with John in hot pursuit. Years
afterwards in that room "Bess, the landlord's daughter," waited
for her lover while the soldiers "tied her up to attention with
many a snickering jest. They bound a musket beside her with the
barrel beneath her breast." Early I formed the habit of giving
people in books a local habitation and a name.

THE HOUSE FROM THE REAR GARDEN

I remember the first time I went alone along the garden path to my grandmother's house. I was wrapped in the red shawl that was a beloved and inseparable part of my childhood. I can still see the dew like diamonds encrusting the heavy grasses and smell the frosty, early morning fragrance mixed with the aroma of breakfast bacon. One afternoon while I was playing near my grandmother's chair—I now spent almost as much time in the big house as in my own—the long rays of the late winter sun cut across the drowsy light of the room and came to rest on the carpet near me. As the slow talk flowed around me and I sat watching the little motes float in and out of the beam, I was conscious of a sadness, a vague hurt that somehow had to do with the shaft of sunlight. I stopped my play for I felt that I was going to cry. Not until years later when I discovered Emily Dickinson's poem

There's a certain slant of light,
On winter afternoons,
That oppresses, like the weight
Of cathedral tunes

did the oppression of that far-off afternoon find words. The "Imperial affliction" comes early and abides however deep the overlay of joy.

I adored my grandmother as did all of her family. Every morning I was taken to see her or went myself. I was the only one with her when she was taken ill for the last time. I remember that I was sitting in her lap outlining a wild rose in turkey red thread. She always had something interesting for me to do, and this wild rose she had drawn on a piece of cardboard and stuck pin holes along the lines for me to sew. As I was busily poking the needle in and out of the holes, she said she was not feeling well and would have to lie down. I sat on the big tester bed beside her until my mother arrived. Mamá grew rapidly worse. All of her children came, and Uncle Hal from Little Rock brought John, his son. He and I were allowed to visit her each day because she wanted to see us. I would pick a rose and take it to her and tell her which bush it had come from. John could sing, and she loved for him to stand by her bed and sing "At the Cross." When she died and I was taken to see her, I thought she looked very beautiful and that the shirred satin lining of her casket was utterly lovely. Somehow, I did not associate death with fear, and all day I gathered roses and took them to her. The remembrance of how she looked came to me when I first read Stephen Phillip's verses:

How beautiful are the dead,
Clear comes each feature,
Satisfied not to be,
Strangely contented.

Like ships the anchor dropped,
Furled every sail is;
Mirrored with all their masts
In a deep water.

Looking through some of my mother's papers, I found a letter that I had dictated to her. Across it mother had written "Verbatim." It was to my mother's best friend:

DEAR ALMA:

Uncle has gone back to Tuscaloosa. Pet went with him as far as Decatur. Father went down town this morning. I stepped over to Mamá's this morning to see my Tante. My Mamá has now gone away, away to the star-land where her children are and Papá looks so sad and dreary and walks up and down the porch and goes in Mamá's room and looks so sad. I went to the funeral with Mother and the casket was very long and lined through with white satin and silk. She was sick a long time and the doctor came to see her so many times and she died in her nightgown, and the funeral was preached at her house. Whenever you mention Mamá's name my Mother weeps. She says she's going to live with Papá and I hear them say: no place like home. We are going to Arkansas after Christmas and Papá is going with us.

I was four years old when we moved over to the big house, and I have lived here ever since. With Papá at that time were his three younger sons, who had been born at Locust Hill— Courtenay, a lawyer; Pearsall, my father's law partner; and John D., a student at The University of Alabama. John D. was a twin; his sister, Mary Wallace, for whom I was named, had died some years before. My Aunt Anne, whom I called Tante, had married John Weakley and lived in Florence, five miles away. Uncle Hal and his wife, Aunt Lila, lived in Little Rock, Arkansas. It had been Uncle Hal's custom every summer to bring his wife and sons (at first there was one and then there were four—John, Hal, Pearsall, and Gordon) to spend a month at Locust Hill. He wanted them to know and love his family and his old home as much as he did. These visits continued after Mamá's death; when the boys grew older, they came alone. It was Aunt Lila who one time said, "Offer any Rather man a ticket to whatever place in the world he would rather go, and he will say 'Locust Hill'!"

Within a year after my grandmother's death, my Uncle Pearsall died. Uncle Hal and John came. John and I again gathered flowers, this time narcissi, and took them to Uncle Pearsall, for we loved him very dearly.

ged for some of his friends to take turns sitting with him.
ime I went to see him I asked to be called if he wanted
ng. One night about eleven o'clock a call came: "Isaiah
tell you he is hungry." Within a few hours he died.

he kitchen was some distance from the house but was con-
with it by a covered brick porch with a long row of
columns. This porch, which held an important place in
nomy of the household, was the scene of many and varied
ies and a gathering place for all the children and servants.
ing was there and a long table where in summer jellies
eserves were brought from the kitchen in big porcelain-
iron kettles and ladled into glasses and jars, cakes iced
e I stood by and licked the knife), desserts put out to cool,
filled, and chimneys cleaned. When the scissors grinder
all the knives to be sharpened were laid out here. What
was to watch him unload his grinder from his back, work
his foot, and put on the sharp edges.

Organ grinders with monkeys or bears were still wander-
rough this part of the country. They caused much excite-
Alp (Papá's St. Bernard) would become almost frantic
ave to be chained while the old Italian ground out his
ing tunes and the little dressed-up monkey doffed his pill-
at, went through his tricks, and then held out his cup for
es. Sometimes he would have a bear that would dance on
wn to my great delight.

On the brick porch there was a big cupboard called the
" where fresh milk and cream and butter were kept. And
ember how the heavy blankets of cream would crinkle and
up as the pans were skimmed. Freezing ice cream was
er ritual, and when the four Arkansas boy-cousins came
for their month's stay each summer all scrambled to get the
her" to lick when it was taken out and the freezer "packed"
ld the cream frozen until mealtime. To keep the peace, all
e losers in the struggle would be given a taste from the
er.

have today of cooking I owe to watching her, for Mary was especially gifted as a cook, while Fanny excelled as a storyteller. The
most absorbing serial that I ever followed was Fanny's day-by-
day account of the doings of three little golden-haired girls—one
dressed in pink satin, one in blue satin, and one in yellow satin.
I would do anything or go anywhere for the privilege of hearing
another episode in their young lives. When Mary washed dishes
and Fanny dried them for her, they would sing duets. How I
longed to take part, to sing one of those high soaring notes of
infinite sweetness! But I merely passed on the stories that had
been read to me or those I had learned at Sunday school. I
remember being very austere with my "best friends" one Sunday.
I was seated on the biscuit block; all of the family were at
church. The atmosphere in the kitchen was completely relaxed,
and Mary and Fanny had been calling on the name of the Lord
with too great a frequency for one fresh from training in the
Presbyterian catechism. From my seat on the biscuit block I
administered the necessary correction: "Though you may escape
punishment from men, the Lord your God will not suffer you to
escape his righteous judgment." Such laughter greeted my re-
proof that I left the kitchen deeply offended.

Another ritual of spring was the taking up of all the wall-
to-wall carpets, having them stored, and putting down in their
stead China matting with its fresh, exciting smell. That matting,
the linen slip covers, spring flowers in vases, and windows wide
open with gently swaying lace curtains gave the house a cool
and different look. Because of the thick brick walls the stored
coolness of winter lingered for a long time, and with the partial
closing of the blinds during the midday heat electric fans were
never needed. Even today Locust Hill does not need air conditioning. Something in the construction of old houses seems to
make them cool.

Equally welcome was the return of the carpets in the
autumn about the time of the raking of leaves. Isaiah, the gard-
ner, when he made great piles of them on the lawn, would let

me jump into them. He was always good to me and would watch over me when I buried myself in them. He would stretch out the carpets on the newly raked grass, and it was great fun to roll over on them when he finished the last beating and sweeping before they were returned to winter quarters. Inside the house, slip covers were removed, draperies were put up, evergreens succeeded flowers, and fires were lighted; then came a warm closed-in feeling that made you think of apples and chestnuts and popcorn. Much the same seasonal ritual still is followed at Locust Hill.

Isaiah was associated with much of my childhood. Having the name of so august a prophet, I always felt somewhat sacrilegious when giving a long call for him, remembering the fate of those biblical children who were too free with another prophet. He worked for us a number of years but eventually heard the call of industry and went to Detroit. Years later when he returned he had mellowed, was deeply religious, and longed for the simple life. Once again he cut grass under the same old trees at Locust

ISAIAH

ISAIAH'S TOOL

Hill and tended the same old rose bus
carefree child, was mistress of the house
sations recalling the past, comparing i
the present. One morning as I stopped
working there was a burst of song fro
Isaiah rose from his work and said, "Th
'work, work, work,' but they has a dif
can't understand their language. I does n
God will be pleased with it."

Isaiah was always punctual and ne
or summer. When two days passed withe
something was wrong. He lived alone;
found him quite ill so had him taken to t
and nurses were good to him, but to keep

I arrar
Each t
anythi
says tc

nected
square
the ec
activit
My sv
and p
lined
(whil
lamps
came,
fun it
it wit

ing tl
ment
and I
wave
box h
penn
the la

"dair
I ren
roll
anotl
over
"feat
to he
of tl
freez

Three steps led from the brick porch to the dining room. How many hours I spent there playing alone, cracking nuts, or with the Arkansas boys eating our midmorning lunches of "mixed-up-stirred" or "bo-hole-y" biscuits and planning for fishing trips, blackberry hunts, or trips to the mountains. "Mixed-up-stirred" was butter and sugar creamed and spread on the two halves of a biscuit; a "bo-hole-y" biscuit had a hole punched partly through the side with the ivory handle of a "case knife" and molasses poured in—a gooey but most delectable mass. When the steps were removed twice a year, many lost treasures came to light. Because the brick porch stood in the line of traffic between the kitchen and the big house, it was often the scene of fights when the Arkansas boys were visiting us. One morning when an older brother knocked his younger brother's hat off, a serious offense and traditional grounds for bitter resentment, a fight followed. In attempting to achieve at least a truce my mother asked if their mother allowed them to fight. The younger one nodded; the older one, with an evident twinge of conscience, cried, "I'll tell you how it is, Aunt Er, us fights and her knows it, but her don't allow it."

A breeze always was blowing through the brick porch, and here in her old age Ghee would sit on summer afternoons nodding and puffing at her little corncob pipe. Meanwhile Alp, the big St. Bernard, and Shadrach, the Irish setter, would stretch out on the cool bricks, and the house would fairly hum with the stillness when most were asleep. Ghee would keep a wary eye on any child who was awake. I would often be in my swing or pulling my crowded doll carriage around the garden or fishing for doodlebugs under the kitchen eaves, intoning "Doodlebug, doodlebug, come out of your hole. Your house is on fire and your children at home." I fished with a broom straw, the end of which had on it, as a lure, a mixture of spit and earth.

Some afternoons Ghee would roast coffee, her special job. My grandfather always had his coffee shipped from New Orleans unroasted, and only a week's supply was ever roasted at one time. He had a pan (the size of the oven) made especially for the purpose. Ghee would cover the bottom of the pan with the green coffee beans, put them in a slow oven, take her seat in front of the oven door, and at short intervals stir the beans with a long-handled wooden spoon. Near the end of the process she would beat egg whites and smear them over the beans. Back in the oven they would go for the glaze. Finally that good smell of freshly roasted coffee pervaded the brick porch.

At four o'clock, naps over, the servant man was dispatched to the ice factory for a watermelon. My grandfather would give the signal; the table would be prepared and plates and forks brought out. When the family gathered and the melon was placed on the table, my grandfather, with due ceremony, cut and served it. If it cracked as the knife was embedded and began to split, laying bare its red heart, it was at just the proper degree of ripeness. As the halves fell apart, he, with the point of his carving knife and a flourishing gesture, would snip out a piece and taste it while all awaited eagerly his judgment on its sweetness. How did you ever attain, I wondered, the position of authority where you could take the first bite out of the heart of a watermelon without having to wait until your piece was handed to you? No one ever selected his or her piece of melon; selection was my grandfather's perogative.

On late winter evenings Aunt Lucy Noe would appear on the brick porch with her bucket of steaming lye hominy for sale. I would begin eating a saucer of it while a bowl of it was being bought. And strawberries never tasted so good as those old Henry would send freshly picked from his garden to the brick porch just in time for breakfast. Much breakage occurred on this porch. Once Aunt Cass, another cook, let fall a tray full of dishes and looking down upon the wreckage mumbled, "The china was just so old and rotten it broke."

Then there was the smokehouse with its dirt floor and rich smell of earthiness mixed with the aroma of smoked hams, bacon, and sugarhouse molasses sent every year by a New

Orleans cousin who also sent bunches of bananas through the years. These were always hung in the cellar. Mother would tell how her young brother came up one day from the cellar and announced that he had eaten twelve! Somehow he survived without a pain.

The wood house was dry smelling from stacks of wood and shavings. It had the largest chimney I had ever seen until I went to England. I could walk into it and see the sky through its top. In my mother's childhood she and her sister and brothers and cousins converted the woodhouse into a theater, and there displayed their histrionic talents in its spacious gloom. There my Uncle Courtenay had a carpenter's bench in my day and would put out tools and make a great show of carpentering. He built for me dolls houses and doll carriages of remarkable design, while my younger uncle carved doll furniture out of cigar boxes and gilded it. One August, my Uncle Courtenay built a sleigh in anticipation of a snow that did not fall until long after the sleigh had rotted into dust.

For some years after our little community had its water-works system, the family continued to follow the biblical injunction, not from piety but from preference, and drank water from its own cistern. We had two cisterns: the little one for utility and the big one for drinking. We thought there was no water so refreshing as that caught from winter rains and kept cool in "the deep-delved earth." When the cistern top was removed, how exciting it was to watch the chain of cups gradually reach its apex and empty in a crystal stream! The brass rims of the cedar bucket were always gleaming, and a little bag of charcoal was attached to the cistern's spout for the water to run through. My grandfather had a definite ritual for the drawing of fresh water; it was an ironclad rule that the first two bucketsful had to be thrown out to insure the disposal of any stale water that might have remained in the cups.

The cellar was another favorite spot. The doors when closed were an excellent sliding place; when opened, the frame furnished a good seat; behind it was the mysterious, shadowy void of the cellar with its croquet sets, old swings, benches, broken chairs, tables, a barrel of Confederate money, pieces of iron, fishing poles and tackle, and very often a bunch of bananas.

In the late afternoons when the Arkansas boys were with us and we were bathed and dressed, around the cellar was a great gathering place. My young uncles, Courtenay and John D., stretched out on the grass, and we children clustered around them. They would tell us stories, play mumble-peg with us, and devise plans of great moment for baseball games with Johnson and Walter Jones from New Jersey, who would be visiting their relatives, the Johnsons.

All of these outlying buildings gave way in time to new facilities for comfort and convenience. When the kitchen was torn down the brick porch went with it, and a service wing was added that included kitchen, pantry, closets, storage space, and a lattice porch. With the installation of central heat the wood and coal houses were out of date; hams no longer being cured on the place, we no longer needed the smokehouse. The carriages, phaetons, and horses have been replaced by a car and garage; a delivery truck brings milk.

More than in most houses old ways lingered on at Locust Hill, as I was forcibly reminded when guests came from compact, space-saving, gadget-filled houses, and I saw my house through their eyes—its large kitchen, its ice-from-the-ice factory refrigerator, and its coal-wood range that I am persuaded cooked better food than any other stove. But I finally capitulated to the god of things as they are and in one of the pantries installed a modern, streamlined kitchen. However, I still send my clothes out to be washed by Emma Lizzie, who is the daughter of one of the "best friends" of my childhood. Until a relatively short time ago clothes were done by Hattie Bohannon, who washed for Mother before I was born, even as her mother, Ellen, had washed for my grandmother. Washing at that time was done on the place. Once there was great excitement when Mamá put her flannel petticoat in the wash, having forgotten that in its pocket (the regular place for keeping large sums of money since there was no bank in the community) was the payroll in currency for the Memphis and Charleston Railroad of which Papá was president. Mother was quickly rushed to bring back the flannel petticoat. Just as she entered the door of the washroom she saw it go under the foaming suds. Rescued, the wet bills were stretched out on a table to dry and weights put on them.

Hattie was a perfect laundress. How well I remember when the clothes were brought in on Saturday afternoons! Nothing ever looked whiter, crisper, more delightfully fresh than the piles of snowy linen laid out on Mother's tester bed, especially the petticoats with their fluted ruffles and dust ruffles that had been rolled and whipped on. They were lace edged and tucked and had compass work between rows of insertions, and there was beading for blue and pink ribbons to be run through. I still have some of those voluminous petticoats. When I went to college I always sent my nicest things home for Hattie to launder, for no one else could do them to suit me.

Across the street were the stables, the carriage houses, and the barn, all enclosed by a whitewashed "Tennessee fence," as we called it, the kind in which the planks made a cross between the top and bottom rails. Every morning by nine o'clock Hal, my grandfather's saddle horse, was hitched at the back gate ready for his use. A very fine animal, Hal had been bought in Kentucky. His air of great superiority and independence suggested awareness of his heritage; when his will and my grandfather's clashed, as they frequently did, my grandmother and later my mother were genuinely concerned, for they knew both the man and the horse. My grandfather was never thrown; so his will in the end must have prevailed.

There were numerous other horses; one, Polly, ran away while Mother was driving her in the phaeton and hence was sold. She was replaced by Lady, a gentle family horse, whom later I was taught to ride. Darby succeeded Hal, who in his old age had to be put out to pasture, and during the latter years of my grandfather's life, Darby, his personal horse, was hitched to his phaeton every morning ready for use. My grandfather and Darby and I were devoted friends. A familiar sight around our little town was Papá driving Darby with me on the seat beside him and Alp III, his big St. Bernard, trotting behind with only the white plume of his tail showing at the back of the phaeton.

On our rides, one of our favorite points of call was at the spring in the heart of town to give Darby a drink of cool, fresh water. It is called the Big Spring because of the great volume of water that flows boldly from under the ledge of limestone rocks to form a wide stream. On the hill above the spring were lovely trees; in fact, it was a beautiful sylvan spot until man tampered with it. On this hill the first settlers of Tuscumbia, Michael Dickson and his family, camped in 1816, having fled from an Indian massacre at Fort Royalton, Tennessee. The main street of the town leads downhill to the spring at the point where it can be forded, except at high water. But Papá never stopped here to let Darby drink; he rode on upstream where the water was freshest. Turning around at that point was rather hazardous, but he enjoyed so doing; it was the signal for me to hold up my feet lest the water come into the phaeton, as it sometimes did. The Big Spring was the scene of many baptizings, with people coming from near and far. The crowd of onlookers stood on the hillside above the spring and watched the converts, each dressed in a white robe securely tied down, who were escorted by two of the brethren to the minister standing out in midstream. Then came the climax when the convert went under the water and came up "washed in the blood of the Lamb." Sometimes when the "Spirit was high" he came up from the water and began to shout; then the brethren had difficulty reaching dry ground with their charge.

We often saw gypsies camped by the Big Spring. They fascinated me intensely and interested my grandfather as well— their swarthy skin, gaily colored clothes, finger rings and dangling earrings, heavy chains and bracelets. Horses and dogs were always in their caravan; the usual iron pots hung beneath their covered wagons.

Hindman's Mill was another favored place. Here Papá took his own corn grown on the place to be ground. There always seems to be something attractive about a mill. Is it because of old songs and stories about jolly millers and their lovely daughters? Or is it the sound of the millstream with the great wheel and the awareness that "the mill will never grind with the water that has passed"? I loved to stand by the millrace, watch the wheel turn, and feel the warm, fragrant meal run through my fingers.

We had cows, too, but I was rather afraid of them and rarely went to the barn. When Daisy, one of the prettiest, had a calf I named it Wreath Rather Wreath because I thought the word "wreath" one of the loveliest I had ever heard. Mother did not care for cows either or for looking to the milking and the butter making. She liked only to print the stars on the fresh cool pats of butter brought to her for inspection. I have often heard her say that when she got to heaven she was going to ask Saint Peter not to put her in the milk and honey section.

Two carriages had their special usages. The old carriage went on picnics, fishing trips, and swimming expeditions, and brought in the tree at Christmas. The other carriage was for special occasions like parties, meeting guests, or going to Florence to see Tante, and for daily afternoon drives that were always formal. We drove to Sheffield, two miles away, and around the park on the bluff of the Tennessee River and back, always meeting the Johnsons in their big double-seated carriage with Mrs. Johnson and her four daughters. The Johnsons also had a trap, and sometimes just the girls would be in that. It had two seats back-to-back so that two of the girls faced forward and two faced backward. Topless, it was considered very dashing. How I longed to ride in it! Then there were the Almons in their surrey, Mrs. Almon and her sister, Mrs. Curry, with their children. And we always met the Halseys in their "surrey with the fringe on top" drawn by two calico ponies and "filled with femininity," as my uncle used to say—five pretty young girls dressed in organdies and muslins, the whole outfit a veritable frou-frou of ruffles and double-ruffles, laces, beading, and fluttering ribbons. I adored them as the quintessence of young ladyhood. They sat behind us in church, and on the Sundays that I was going to "stay to church," I would take a tiny bunch of flowers with me and quickly turn and give it to the one of my choice. In the winter it was the Johnson young ladies that I admired most. I can see them now walking up the church aisle, arrayed in furs and carrying muffs with bunches of artificial violets pinned on them. One of them had a hat with a crown that I thought was made of popcorn. Two other ladies we always would see on our drives were very dressy, drove themselves, and rode in a phaeton with the top half back, but for some reason we did not know them. It was rumored that one of them had caused the death of her husband. These regulars that we met were the only ones for whom a late afternoon drive was part of the day's routine.

Papá and Mama

PAPÁ WAS BORN IN SOMMERVILLE, ALABAMA, ON JANUARY 7, 1823. His mother died when he was four years old, and my great-grandfather's second marriage brought no happiness to his only child. He was often taken by his father on journeys to the legislative halls of the state capital, then Tuscaloosa, where his father had been a member of the legislature for many years. Papá remembered those visits vividly. There he ate his first oyster and saw his first steamboats, *The Ivanhoe* and *The Sun*. When eleven he accompanied his father on horseback to Tuscaloosa, and he loved to tell how on that trip he saw the famous Peggy O'Neill. On the return journey his father put him in the charge of a friend. This gentleman told him to watch for a coach that they would soon be passing. Its occupants would be Peggy O'Neill and her husband, Major Eaton, who had been Secretary of War in Andrew Jackson's Cabinet and was then going to Florida as governor general. Papá was thrilled as they passed the coach and Major Eaton took off his hat and the famous Peggy O'Neill bowed to the gentleman and little boy on horseback. Papá loved a stagecoach. He would tell how when a young boy he and his friends would go to the Court House Square about the time the stagecoach was due; how excited he became at the blare of the horn in the distance, the first sight of the horses and the coach-and-four dashing down the street until the driver, with a flourish of his whip, suddenly drew rein in front of the Court House door. At that time the height of his ambition was to be a stage-coach driver himself.

JOHN D. RATHER,
AGE TWENTY-FIVE

LETITIA PEARSALL RATHER

When he was thirteen and on his way to enter the University of Tennessee, the boat carrying him to Knoxville ran aground on a sand bar just below the city, and the passengers were forced to walk the remaining distance. On the journey he got into conversation with a man who told him he was going to Knoxville to be imprisoned for debt. Papá was so horrified that he gave the man the forty dollars necessary to pay himself out. Later Papá read law under Judge Daniel Coleman of Athens, Alabama. He was one of a group of whom all became prominent in state affairs.

Before the war Papá served a number of terms in the state legislature and later in the senate, though I often heard him say that he had never asked a man to vote for him and never would. He withdrew from politics when campaign methods changed. Famous as a presiding officer, public speaker, and parliamentarian, he was elected Speaker of the House when twenty-eight years of age and President of the Senate when thirty-six. During his term of office it became his duty to preside over the called meeting of the senate immediately preceding the secession of the state. A lawyer, he served as circuit judge during the war, was on General Roddy's staff, and was a general in the state militia. After moving to Tuscumbia, he became a partner in the law firm of Moore and Rather; he was the first president of the North Alabama Bar Association, organized in Huntsville, May 22, 1868, antedating the organization of the Alabama Bar Association by ten years; and he was a member of the Constitutional Convention of 1875.

He left the practice of law to become president of the Memphis and Charleston Railroad, which eventually became a part of the Southern Railway System. For a number of years he had been a stockholder and director, as had his father before him, but he retired early from the presidency as he felt that its duties necessitated too much time away from his family. There were occasional trips to New York for directors' meetings and, when attending those meetings, he usually was invited out socially. On one such occasion a friend invited him for lunch at the Astor Hotel saying, "It's *the place* for lunch now in New York. We have Negro waiters there, and I want you to see what we have done with them." On reaching the dining room the head waiter recognized my grandfather, burst into tears, and put his arms around him saying, "Oh, Mars John, I'm so glad to see you." Upon seating Papá and his friend, he plied them with the choicest items on the menu and paid them constant attention. In talking with Henry, Papá asked, "Are you telling these other waiters that I was your old master?" "Yes, sir, and I'm proud to show you off." Whereupon his friend turned to my grandfather and said, "I don't understand it. This man belonged to you, and look what he thinks of you! I just can't understand it." Papá laid his hand on the director's shoulder saying, "What's more, my friend, you never will."

Mother has told me how every winter evening when Papá was not away from home the candle stand would be placed in front of the fire, the children would be seated around it, and as Mamá sewed Papá would read to them—Shakespeare, Thackeray, Scott, Byron, Gibbon, Prescott, Hawthorne, Washington Irving, and others. He had a fine speaking voice and was unusually gifted in reading aloud. One of his director friends in New York said it was a luxury to hear him read even so dry a thing as a report. My mother and uncle were likewise gifted. Perhaps because of these evenings under the lamplight, his children developed a great love of reading. He was very fond of geography and often sang to me the boundaries of countries as he had been taught to do when a little boy at school—of Russia, for instance:

THE WHITE SEA   THE BLACK SEA   THE SEA OF AZOV   THE SEA OF AZOV

One felt humiliated to return from a trip, however short, unable to review the counties, states, and towns visited, to give the names of rivers crossed, and to describe the general look of the countryside. All famous events, national and international, major historical dates, and birthdays of famous men were taken note of, discussed, usually at the table, and in some way celebrated. Even today when I date a letter or check I am struck by the way those anniversaries come automatically to mind.

Papá loved good clothes and wore them. In his latter years he always wore a Prince Albert for weddings and church services. From New York he would bring lovely furs and shawls and scarfs and jewelry to his wife and daughters, and always books. I remember Mother telling about the English walking jackets he once brought her and her sister. Papá was very orderly and methodical about everything, even to keeping his watch in time with the sun and the almanac. I used to walk up and down the long porch with him in the evenings when he timed his watch with the setting sun, and we would close the blinds of the windows opening on the porch while the gardener went the rounds closing the others. The gardener's first job in the morning was to open them and let in the early morning freshness. When the laundry was brought in, I thought it great fun to be allowed to help put away Papá's shirts, collars, and handkerchiefs, for he had a certain ritual that had to be followed. All of the clean shirts in the drawer had to be taken out, the fresh ones put on the bottom, and the others laid on top; so, all got equal wear. Courtenay, who was reading at life of Napoleon, announced one day at the table that Napoleon had had his clothes so arranged. All accused Papá of copying the Emperor, but he denied any such imitation.

Papá was the dominant figure of the family, deeply loved and revered by all his children and grandchildren. He was a man of sound judgment, unquestioned integrity, and brilliant mind, charming in manner and delightful in conversation, full of good stories and wise observations. Today we would say that he had

JOHN D. RATHER, AGE EIGHTY-TWO

charisma. One of my earliest recollections is riding on his foot or being trotted on his knee while he sang to me.

> The lady bird sat in the rose's heart
> And laughed with pride and scorn
> To see the little ant passing by
> Trundling a grain of corn.

was one of my favorites; I have never heard it since. Sometimes he recited "My name is Norval. On the Grampian Hills my father feeds his flock"—a passage from *Douglas*, John Home's famous play, in which as a young man in Sommerville Papá had played the title role. And

> Maid of Athens 'ere we part
> Give, oh give me back my heart.

was another poem I remember hearing him recite. Sometimes in a lighter mood he would sing:

> Old Dan'l Tucker was a mighty mean man,
> He used to ride old Darby Rand.
> He rode him down to the foot of the hill,
> And if he hasn't gotten back he's down there still.
> Get out the way, Get out the way, Old Dan'l Tucker,
> You're too late to get your supper.

and other folk songs.

Judge Henry C. Jones was Papá's brother-in-law by his first marriage, and he and Papá were devoted friends. Every few weeks "Uncle Henry," as all the family affectionately called him, would ride over on horseback from Florence, about five miles away, to spend the day. As those two fondly reminisced, I played on the floor near their chairs and delighted in their stories. There was one about a trip made out west on horseback in the 1850's that they often told and that always fascinated me. They were curious to see the newly developing country that was attracting many settlers. Mother said that even in her childhood any day you could see groups of "movers" in their big wagons with white canvas-covered, barrel-shaped tops pass through the town. Dallas, Texas, was a magnet for Papá and Uncle Henry. They had various experiences along the way, for the country was wild; there were few settlements, the roads were rough and poorly marked, and most of the streams had to be forded. Once Uncle Henry went ahead in crossing a stream and got in water so deep that he and his horse parted company while his saddlebags, filled with gold dollars, headed downstream. Papá, an excellent swimmer, ran downstream, plunged in, and caught the saddlebags with his teeth just as they were going under.

On reaching Dallas the lawyers were interested in seeing how justice was administered in this frontier town. I remember how Papá described the log house in which court was held and how, when they entered the courtroom, the judge was sitting behind a large "goodsbox" used as a desk with a double-barreled shotgun atop it—I suppose as either a warning or a weapon. On the return trip when they came upon a certain fork in the road, they disagreed on which direction to take. Neither would budge. With no ill feelings each followed his own judgment. There in the wilderness they shook hands, said good-bye, and departed on their separate ways. At this point they invariably ended the story. But soon some listener would always ask, "Which one was right?" Then Uncle Henry would screw up his face and say, "Yeh, Yeh, I got down into Mexico and fell among Indians and had a hard time getting home."

Almost every week Uncle Press Keyes, another brother-in-law, would walk over from Sheffield, a mile distant, to spend the day. Usually someone would happen to see him coming and announce with pleasure: "Here comes Uncle Press!"—a tall slender figure, head slightly bowed as if in meditation, walking with measured stride. He had been a newspaper man in Montgomery, Alabama, and had come to this part of the state with the group of Montgomery men who were among the founders of

Sheffield. A dreamer, his talk was always of airplanes, I remember, or some utopian dream for making the world a better place. Mother was a great favorite of his, and he had written a charming poem to her on her wedding day. He had a beautiful daughter whom he had named Amaranth, but she was called Ammie. She was a contemporary of mother and of Tante; they were devoted to her.

When I reached school age, Papá drove me to school every morning, came for me at noon, and brought me home in the afternoon. Punctuality being a fetish with him, I was never late. He always gave me a "last call" in the mornings, and if I did not respond immediately but continued to dawdle as children will, he did not say anything and did not whip up his horse but held the same pace to which Darby had been trained, while I fidgeted on the seat beside him. If I asked, "Can't Darby go a little faster?" he made no reply but kept on with what he was saying. It was some time before I realized that he would never let me be late, although he timed it so we just got "under the wire." My teachers said it was unnecessary ever to consult the clock as to the time to dismiss school, for the sight of General Rather's horse and phaeton was timepiece enough. He was always there on the stroke of three. By the time I reached home, I knew all the happenings of the day. When Mother communicated some piece of news I usually replied, "I know it; Papá told me." Once at the table my family cried out with astonishment when I announced that I had seen "a jackass." "Yes," Papá said, "she asked what it was and I told her." There was no further comment. There were always two trips a day to the post office, regardless of where else we went. One was for the morning mail and the other was timed for the exact moment in the afternoon when his favorite newspaper, *The Louisville Courier Journal*, would be put in his box.

In a recent letter a friend mentioned my grandfather and went on to say, "I remember him especially at church and how I was impressed by his great dignity and his courtly manner in speaking, even to me, a little boy." Although a student of the

Bible, Papá never united with the church because of certain dogma that he could not honestly say he believed. Whenever invited to attend a revival in the community, he would reply, "I thank you for the invitation, but I will not go and be made an object of sin." Once his son Courtenay persuaded him to go to hear Sam Jones, a noted evangelist of the day. In the course of the sermon Mr. Jones began asking personal questions and pointing at random over the congregation. When he asked, "Are your debts paid?" his finger pointed directly at Papá! Courtenay wanted to tell Mr. Jones, "If you look on top of the wardrobe you will find a receipt for every bill."

My grandmother (Mamá) was Letitia Pearsall, one of the five Pearsall sisters of Pond Creek Plantation, all noted for their good looks, sparkling humor, and charm. Her father was Edward Pearsall, who died before the Civil War. A man of deep religious convictions, he was famed for his honesty. "Let honest Ned pay it," a saying often applied to him, originated when he assumed payment of a thirty thousand dollar note when all the other signatories reneged. There is a charming story of his purchase of a horse from a group of itinerant horse traders. The horse was priced at one hundred dollars; he considered that too much and offered seventy-five dollars, which was accepted. The following year when the traders returned he searched them out, said they were right about the value of the horse, and gave them the additional twenty-five dollars. Although a slave owner, it was his custom to pay wages to his personal and house servants, and he paid them in gold. When the war ended, Maria, my great-grandmother's personal maid, would not leave her or the plantation; neither would her children, and they continued their services to my great-grandmother until her death. Later, when the plantation went out of the hands of the family, Maria, who had held the purse strings for her children, began to buy up some of the acreage. Had she not said, "I wants to live where Mistess lived, and to drink the water what Mistess drunk, and I wants to sleep where Mistess sleeps"? She was buried in the family burying ground, carried to her last resting place by her six sons, who had asked the privilege of doing the same for my great-grandmother. Even today some of Maria's descendants live on their holdings and are very well-to-do.

But Maria's youngest son, Ben, chose a very different way of life. Whether parental discipline had been too severe or an atavistic instinct too strong, Ben, after his mother's death, deserted the forty acres she had left him and took to the road. As a little girl I remember seeing him once when he came by the house and stopped at the back gate, a blanket-draped figure ready for travel. He was straight, strong, and clean-limbed. Fleet as a

BEN

deer, he could cover many miles in a day's walk. He refused to wear more clothes than a loincloth and a blanket draped over his shoulders. He would disappear down the big road, and for months no one would know of his whereabouts. On his return he never told of his travels.

During his absences his land grew up in plum thickets and saplings. He allowed no one to cultivate it. At last his wanderings stopped. His roots held him to the land, and he settled down on his acreage, but not to cultivate it. He associated less and less with people, including his own family. His little cabin he filled with dried cornstalks, brush, and hay foraged from the fields. Samson-like, he felt that his great strength lay in his hair and defied anyone to cut it while he slept; it was in no danger during his waking hours. His flesh he kept greased, and it shone in the sun like polished ebony. Clad only in a loincloth and lei of knotted rags, he would often appear suddenly from bush or thicket and startle the unsuspecting traveler. So he came to be feared as the "crazy wildman," but he was never known to harm anyone. His greetings were usually kind, even stately.

My uncle would drive out to see him occasionally and take him clothes that he would wear for a time. My uncle was the only person from whom he would accept anything or whose advice he would consider. Once Uncle took me and some of my friends to see Ben. As we approached his place, he suddenly appeared from a plum thicket and stood in the way. He knew at once who I was and called my name and that of my mother. When I introduced my friends, he put his hand over his heart, bowed from the waist, and said: "I am very pleased to meet you." One of the girls was Miss Sloan, and he immediately asked her if she were related to the Mr. Sloan of New Jersey who had been principal of the Tuscumbia Female Seminary. Turning to me, he remarked: "That's where your grandmother went to school in '51. I used to go in and take her presents from the plantation."

He showed us over his place—the little house among the peach and plum trees and the cave he had dug, cone-shaped, and just large enough at the bottom for one person to sit in. In it he tended a fire that he never let go out. There he seared the wild game that he killed, for he lived exclusively by foraging. There was an old Studebaker wagon under a tree that he said had stood there for thirty years. Intact, it yet had the look of burned paper just before it disintegrates. He had dug trenches for his water supply and had built dry-rock walls in coffin shapes where he told us he took naps. The rock walls were to keep out the snakes. Ben had a large and ugly scar on one leg from a rat bite, he declared. He had plastered the wound with red clay, and its healing powers seemed to have been perfect.

The path to his cave had a barricade on either side made of old weathered logs, broken branches of trees, and cornstalks. As he directed us to go down the path, and his magnificent body with only the loincloth and the lei of knotted rags closed up the entrance, I felt that I was truly on a magic carpet and had landed in Africa. Halfway down the path he paused, laid his hand on the barricade, and, looking up through an opening in the scrub oak and plum trees, said, "This is where I stand every evening and watch the sun go down."

Although very old, Ben was still erect and free in movement, but soon after our visit my uncle persuaded him to let one of his nephews cultivate his land in exchange for furnishing him his meals. Ben laid down the conditions that should govern this arrangement. There was to be no intercourse between him and his nephew, though Ben felt no dislike for him; he simply wanted to be let alone. Food sufficient for each day was to be placed under a certain tree, and Ben would get it when he wanted it. Months passed and the plan worked beautifully. Then one day the nephew saw that rations for three days had gone untouched. Feeling that Ben was in trouble, he soon found him very ill of pneumonia. Unresisting, Ben was taken to his nephew's house and ministered to, and there he died. Those at the funeral found it strange to see Ben dressed and lying in a narrow coffin.

At Boxwood, the plantation home of her oldest sister, Mrs. Samuel Elliott, Mamá met Papá, and there is a chair in our parlor associated with that meeting. My great-grandfather Rather bought the chair in Memphis, Tennessee, where he had gone to purchase plantation supplies. On his return to his Morgan County plantation he left the boat at South Florence and transferred to the Tuscumbia, Courtland, and Decatur Railroad and had the chair placed in his coach. At that time the seats on the train were "split-bottom" chairs and when Miss Letitia Pearsall, going to visit her sister at Boxwood, got on the train, he, knowing who she was, insisted that she sit in his more comfortable chair. That visit to Boxwood resulted in her getting not only the chair but his son as well.

Mamá came to Locust Hill from a home in ashes. She and her maid, Ghee, and three young children were alone in their plantation home when a federal soldier entered, put the point of his bayonet at her breast, and demanded any money or any soldiers she might be secreting. She drew herself up to her full height, looked him in the eye, and dismissed him with the scornful words, "You coward." He fled but returned with a squad of soldiers and burned the house, cutting up rosewood furniture to start the fire. With her children and maid, she escaped to the overseer's house. Everything in the smokehouse as well as all the stock and other food stuffs having been confiscated, there was nothing for her young children; she wrote a note to the commanding officer asking for the return of two cows. He sent her one. The overseer fortunately had sweet potatoes—not only were they eaten, he also resourcefully roasted some of them until completely crisp and used them after they were ground for making a coffee substitute.

For a number of years after the close of the war, life in the South was still circumscribed and barren; money was scarce and goods hard to come by. Even a dime in a boy's pocket was a rare possession with which he had to finance himself indefinitely. I have heard my Uncle John D. say that when as a child he had a dime or a quarter in his pocket he would go to stores in town and whenever he saw any article priced at ten or twenty-five cents he would finger his coin and say to himself, "I could buy this," "I could buy that," but the actual spending of it was cause for great concern and much pondering.

But Mamá had imagination and was gifted with an inventiveness that she used in making her home a delightful and an interesting place in which to live and to enjoy living. Her stepsons adored her, as later all of her own children did. She was a genius with children and during her life had ample opportunity to express it. In 1874 a tornado swept through Tuscumbia destroying homes, churches, and public buildings, and leaving eleven dead. Among them was Mamá's youngest, and beloved, sister, Mrs. Moore, and two of her four daughters. The house in which they lived was a large brick one at the head of the main street of the town; all that was left of it was the frame of the front doorway. The other two daughters, Susie and Anne Lee, were seriously injured; Mamá took them, nursed them back to health, and reared them until they were ready for boarding school. On the death of her oldest sister, Mrs. Elliott, of Boxwood, she took her sister's daughters, Anne and Catherine, to live with her until they, too, were ready to go off to school.

Miss Rosa Belle, the last of the Warren family, who were dear friends of the Rathers, often came to see me during the latter years of her life. As a child and as a young woman she had been an almost daily visitor to Locust Hill. Frequently on visits to me she would say, "How I love to see you sit in that chair by the south window in the library, the one in which your grandmother sat and your mother. Your grandmother was regal looking; she was tall and stately, and she sang beautifully. The General often said he would rather hear her sing than Materna or Jennie Lind. As she sat there serene and gentle, she always had a book in her hand, or a piece of sewing—a thread-cambric ruffle she was rolling and whipping, or a bit of hemstitching— and what a merry laugh! It made you feel gay to hear it, so full was it of genuine enjoyment." Mamá not only had a beautiful voice; she played the piano and the harp, and she grounded her sons in Latin for their university days. Her Chickering piano, given to her by my grandfather in 1857, is still in the parlor, and there are two volumes of the popular songs of her youth bound in red morocco, the covers stamped in a gold design. Inside is her name and the date 1850. On various songs are schoolgirl comments and names of her friends. A part of the family ritual was gathering around the piano while she played and sang to them and taught them to sing. Two of her children were musical—my mother and Tante. She had a delightful sense of humor and great capacity for enjoyment, as did her husband. Together they passed on these traits to their children, heaped up and running over. There was no lack of family sharing of the daily comedy of things.

The night the twins were born, my mother and some of the other children were sleeping in the nursery, and one of them had

THE TWINS, MARY WALLACE AND JOHN D., JR.

GHEE

croup. Mother woke up to see Ghee bending over the fire and making one of her concoctions for croup. While slowly stirring the mixture she said, "You've got a mighty fine little brother downstairs." After a long pause she added, "The girl is the larger." By then the nursery had waked up, and there was great jubilation—"Another one to play ball with us! Another one to go to Decatur!" From that hour John D. was Ghee's special charge and her favorite of all the children. When he went off to the University, Mamá discovered Ghee behind the door weeping bitterly. "If it wasn't for his good," she said, "me wouldn't even try to stand it. I love him better than my own children."

In Mother's reminiscences about her childhood, the four girl cousins played a prominent part and, after the twins were born, she and Susie each claimed one as their special pet. Mother claimed Mary Wallace and Susie claimed John D. His relatives were so numerous and varied that John D. had difficulty separating relationships and, to her great delight, called Susie, "my sister-cousin-aunt Sue." She liked to show off her sweet voice and would throw her arm rapturously around the little fellow and ask, "What do you want your sister-cousin-aunt Sue to sing to you?" With an adoring smile he would look up and say, "Nothing." When John D. was a child he was so absorbed in daydreaming and in his play that it was difficult to nourish him properly. Mamá devised a plan to make a game of the food on his plate. She printed stars and half-moons on his mashed potatoes as she told him the names and stories of the heavenly bodies. She would cut meat in the shape of states or countries and give the names of rivers to the little valleys between the foods. When Mamá read aloud to him, mythology was a favored subject, and on his birthday her gift to him was the "Midas Touch." When he washed his face that morning a shiny dime flashed in the bowl on the washstand, another under his napkin, one under his glass of milk, and still another under his plate when he had finished eating all that was on it.

When the children were growing up, it was the family custom for each child to recite a Bible verse at the breakfast table. One morning Courtenay was unprepared; he was excused in order to learn one. When called on after his return to the table, he cried, "And they did all eat and were filled." It was always a moot question as to whether he had planned it that way or had accidentally come upon the apt quotation, for Courtenay was one of the more original of the children and quite unpredictable. Papá would often say, "If he should drown, we would have to look for him upstream." Once John D., home from Sunday school and giving his mother an account of what happened, said that the superintendent had called on all the children for Bible verses. "And did you say one, darling?" his mother asked. "No, I didn't." "But you know so many, surely you remembered 'The Lord is my shepherd'?" "Yes, I knew it, but I thought it had been run in the ground, and I wouldn't say it." Once in great seriousness he asked his father, "Am I a bore?" John D. was a great lover of Bible stories and, every night after being undressed, he would climb up on the big four-poster bed and tell one of his favorites. When Jonah was chosen he would dramatize Jonah's expulsion from the whale's belly by turning a somersault onto the trundle bed. Every night he prayed especially for his sisters, Ella and Anne. He asked the Lord to keep them on the right track and if they got off to "let Jesus be the construction train and put them back on."

Once the Presbyterian church caught fire, and when my grandfather arrived on the scene he found John D. kneeling in the middle of the street praying in a loud voice, "Oh, God, please don't let it burn. It is my house of worship, my place of refuge." When in later years he heard this prayer attributed to him, he always added, "And it didn't burn." Mary Wallace, John D.'s twin sister, died when she was five years old and was buried on Christmas Eve. John D. was inconsolable, and the next day when his presents were given to him, he said, "Take them away until I get over this."

Mamá was a charming hostess, and the tradition of hospitality at Locust Hill began with her. Mother has told me how especially in summer the house overflowed with guests—girl friends and girl cousins of the older boys, friends of my grandfather and of his father, her own sisters and brothers. From far and near all gravitated to Locust Hill sure of a warm welcome. Later the daughters-in-law and the grandchildren came, and friends of my mother and Tante. There were many unexpected guests for meals as well as house guests. Ghee was a great help

ELLA RATHER

ANNE RATHER

to Mamá with all of this company, especially in seeing that the other servants attended to their duties, which were many. Ghee never allowed the family standard to be lowered under any circumstances; in fact, she was the self-appointed guardian of all family mores. Even my grandfather was not exempt from her appraising eye. When mother or Tante consulted her on any matter of procedure or deportment, hers was the final word if she replied, "Your grandmother would never have done it."

It is staggering to think of how much work this hospitality put upon the servants without waterworks, central heating, and electricity. They had to carry hot and cold water up and down stairs, clean and trim lamps, and in winter keep fires glowing all day and into the night. Mother remembered one cook who was never daunted by the arrival of an unexpected guest but, when the news was relayed to the kitchen, would always respond with the enticing suggestion, "Me can give them nice hot corn bread and cool butter." If her suggestion was not accepted, she was always ready to "knock up a cake." About the time olives were becoming popular but were still unknown in Tuscumbia, Tante, returning from a trip, brought some with her and forthwith gave a dinner party to introduce them. The meal progressed to its close, but the olives were never passed. Keenly disappointed, Tante, after the guests had gone, asked Ghee what had happened. "Anne Rather, I tasted them things and they wasn't fit to eat, and I wouldn't let them be passed at Miss Letitia's table."

Of all the children Anne was the independent and dauntless one. Once when a very young child she went alone across the street into the pasture and was rescued as she stood shaking her small fist at a cow charging towards her. The family accused her of always wearing her fighting clothes because she was born during the war. Many years later in Birmingham her chauffeur stopped her car in front of a downtown office building in which she had an appointment. It was a "no parking" area, and a policeman standing nearby preemptorily ordered the chauffeur to "Move on!" Tante ordered him to stop and had the policeman called to the car. "I want you to know that I was not going to park my car, I was only getting out for an appointment," she said. "I have as much respect for the law as you have. My grandfather was a member of the Second Constitutional Convention of Alabama, my father of the third, my husband and brother-in-law of the fourth, and I expect to be a member of the next one." "Madame, park your car wherever you please" was the policeman's reply. When Tante came home for lunch on her first day at school, she announced that none of the girls would sit with Rosa Bressler because she was a Jewess. Papá immediately said to her, "My daughter, when you return to school, go to your teacher and tell her that you would like to have Rosa Bressler for a deskmate." And so Tante did and made a friend.

I have been told that when she was a young girl the boys flocked around her. One of them, a likable but irresponsible youth, became extremely attentive. Papá, aware of this, told his daughter that she must not become interested in him because she could never marry him. Once when the young man tried to kiss her she exclaimed, "You can't do that because my father says I can never marry you." She had another beau who sent her a lovely watch for a Christmas present, which Papá told her she could not accept. When next John Weakley called, she returned the watch and informed him, "Father says I cannot accept this." He took it back and retorted, "You will some day." A year or two later it was his present to her when they were married.

Tante was a graduate of Price's College for Young Ladies in Nashville, Tennessee. On her one hundredth birthday, February 18, 1965, she received a telegram of congratulations from the Price family, and she quoted to me the last sentence of her graduation essay, which was a plea for higher education of women. The following year she took a postgraduate course at Vanderbilt University, one of the first women to be granted that privilege. To celebrate her centennial a majority of her nephews and their wives gathered in Birmingham at the invitation of Pratt and Kathleen Rather to do her honor. At the cocktail party in her apartment, which she entered into with great spirit, she said, "I am sitting here felicitating myself on eleven nephews—all fine, educated Christian gentlemen who have done well in their chosen fields."

Mother and Tante, when young ladies, usually went to Memphis for their best dresses, and Kreamer's, was their favorite store. One autumn they saw displayed in Kreamer's window a gorgeous dress of red velvet with a train and an Elizabethan collar. Down the front was a panel of white satin embroidered in crimson poppies. They looked at it longingly. Their friend Lucy Abernathy was to be married that autumn, and she, too, went to Memphis for her clothes. There was great excitement when she returned home with the red velvet dress in her trousseau. She was the friend who when a young man would ask her to dance always conditioned her acceptance with, "If you hold me at the proper distance."

Later the style center for this part of the country shifted to Louisville, Kentucky, with its numerous shopping agents, fine stores, tailors, and modistes. Those agents made a big business of shopping for families in outlying districts. You went to Louisville and engaged a shopping agent, had a form made to your size and measurements, and did the rest by mail. These agents continued in business until after World War I. I can remember the big envelopes of samples that would come with the description of how each piece of material would be made up and the trimmings to be used. Julius Winter was the name of the favored tailor and Madame Dhority the favored modiste. And what excitement there was when the box arrived with the dress and it was tried on. Was it becoming? Did it fit? Would it have to be sent back for alterations? I remember the proud day when I had my first Louisville-made dress. Miss Vassie Shouse was the agent who would have children's clothes made. It was a little pink striped silk, and I thought it very beautiful and stylish.

The services of these agents were not limited to suits and dresses; they would send all manner of things on approval—

hats, gloves, bags, hose, underwear, linens, handkerchiefs, even pins (the good English kind), and fancy groceries and ices, cakes, candies, and favors for parties. I remember receptions and parties that mother had and the beautiful, as well as delicious, refreshments that came from Louisville. Stocks in small town stores were limited in quantity and quality, and this service saved many trips to nearby cities.

Papá and Mamá usually went away for a month the latter part of the summer and took John D., their youngest, with them; the other children were left in Ghee's care. Papá suffered from hay fever. After trying a number of resorts in the Carolinas, he heard of Petoskey on Little Traverse Bay in northern Michigan as a refuge for hay fever victims. The climate proved to be so delightful and so effective that they went every year. They made many friends in Petoskey, and Papá became president of the Hay Fever Club that flourished in those days. Mamá said she was sure he was elected president because he could sneeze the loudest. He continued going there every summer for the rest of his life, and he lived to be eighty-seven. After Mamá's death my Uncle John D. always accompanied him.

PORTRAIT OF JOHN D. RATHER ABOVE THE
MANTEL IN THE LIBRARY

THE LIBRARY AS SEEN FROM THE OUTSIDE ENTRANCE

THE PARLOR TO THE LEFT OF THE ENTRANCE

THE CHICKERING PIANO IN THE PARLOR

THE PARLOR AS SEEN FROM THE HALL ENTRANCE

THE DOWNSTAIRS BEDROOM

THE HALL

THE DINING ROOM

Friends of
Long Ago

IN SUCH A LARGE HOUSEHOLD OF CHILDREN THE FAMILY
physician played an intimate and important part, and Mamá
counted as her friend as well as her physician dear old Dr. Desprez. A devout Catholic, he was a man of deep piety who
prefaced every prescription or dose of medicine with "Please
Goodness" or "With God's blessing I will try this." If there was
a serious illness in the family, Dr. Desprez would always knock
on the door at midnight and say, "I want to see my patient at
the turn of the night." Of few words and a strict code of profes-
sional ethics, he would reply to any casual inquiry about his
patients, "It is none of your business." Dr. Desprez was born in
Paris of a family of intense royalists, his uncle having been tutor
of the Dauphin at the Court of Louis XVI. When he was young
his father and uncle escaped with him from France and went to
Ireland. Among the heirlooms treasured by his descendants is the
old tricolor they used as a disguise in their escape and a beautiful
ivory miniature of the uncle. In Ireland Dr. Desprez grew up,
studied medicine, and married Miss Ruxton of Ardee House in
County Louth. They came to New Orleans and then to Tuscumbia in the late 1850's, where he died of yellow fever while min-
istering to the stricken victims of the epidemic that swept the
community in 1880. When I visited Ardee House in Ireland
several years ago, I admired its rooms with their beautiful
plaster-work ceilings and cornices and the stairway with its
mullioned window at the landing. I easily imagined the young

bride coming down those steps to join her French born doctor, who was to minister to my ancestors in Alabama.

Knowing the affection in which he had been held by my grandmother and, in fact, by the whole family (the children called him "Please Goodness"), his granddaughter gave my mother a copy of this prayer, which, after his death, she had found written in his prescription book:

> Thou great Bestower of health, strength, and comfort, grant a blessing on the professional duties in which I may this day engage. Give me judgment to discern disease and skill to treat it. Crown with favor the means that may be devised for recovery, for with thy assistance the humblest instrument will succeed, as without it the ablest is unavailing.
>
> Save me from all sordid motives and endow me with the spirit of pity and liberality towards the poor; tenderness and sympathy towards all that I may weep with those that weep and rejoice with those that rejoice.
>
> And satisfy their souls as well as their bodies. Let faith and patience have their perfect work as well as every Christian virtue they are called to exercise, so that in the gracious healing of thy Providence, they may see it has been good for them to have been affected.

Another friend who frequented Locust Hill in the early days was Major David Deshler, a native of Germantown, Pennsylvania. He came to Tuscumbia as engineer for the old Tuscumbia, Courtland, and Decatur Railroad, the second to be built in the United States. It was a short line, and its purpose was to transport cotton around the Muscle Shoals in the Tennessee River, thereby giving farmers of this section easier access to the great cotton ports of Memphis and New Orleans. Later, when the railroad went into the hands of a receiver, he bought it outright.

Major Deshler made Tuscumbia his home, and when the building of the Memphis and Charleston Railroad was decided upon he was chosen as engineer for the project. The day on which the road was completed he made the following entry in his diary:

March 27th, 1857
"The last rail laid"
Memphis and Charleston united! It is now over a quarter of a century since the inception of the project of uniting the Mississippi at Memphis with the Atlantic at Charleston by Rail, and just now—this day—is it accomplished.

The men who conceived this idea and commenced the work were not permitted to bring it to a conclusion.

A large portion of those spirits whose boldness in enterprize subjected them to a suspicion of having been mad have fallen by the way, and have been almost, if not entirely forgotten, whilst a few remain to witness and rejoice in the realization of their early dreams.

Those upon whom has fallen the task of carrying out to completion the work so early begun, have great reason for self gratulation, and deserve all the applause that can be bestowed by a grateful and appreciating community. Yet so far as inward feeling goes, the few who yet survive —who were at the beginning and now see the end— experience that peculiar and thrilling joy and appreciation in the consummation which only those so situated can properly comprehend.

The great work is now accomplished; and our favored Tennessee Valley is fairly *unlocked* so that we have free access to the South Atlantic ports, on the one hand, and to the "Father of Waters" on the other. Who will say we are not blessed?

Shortly after the completion of the railroad, plans were made to symbolize this uniting of Memphis with Charleston by having trains leave simultaneously from the two cities, each carrying a barrel of water—one from the Mississippi River and one from the Atlantic Ocean. At the end of their journeys ceremonies were lavishly planned and executed for this "marriage of the waters," as it was called.

A poignant reminder of this celebration came to Mother's friend Lucy Abernathy Baker who, like all women, dreaded the approach of age and, like all women, attempted to thwart time. In so doing she decided, among other ruses, to adopt a certain age and not admit, at least to herself, any additional years. One brilliant May Day morning she went into the garden and greeted "Uncle Charles," who had worked for her family for many years, "Uncle Charles, this is my birthday, and I am thirty-two years old." He looked up at her and said, "That won't do, 'cause I remember the day you was born. The new train was comin' through here and your Pa was mighty anxious to go to the celebration in Memphis, and he was goin' to take me on the train with him, but you was comin', and he didn't know how it was goin' to be. Sho' nuff, you come the very day the train got here and we couldn't go. That was the first day of May, 1857." Lucy Abernathy Baker could only reply, "I see, Uncle Charles, you know more about it than I do."

Major Deshler had two sons, both of whom he sent to West Point. One was drowned while a student there; the other became the youngest brigadier general in the Confederate army and was killed at the Battle of Chicamauga. His death broke the old man's heart. My grandfather and Major Deshler were devoted friends, and he was loved by the entire family. The last act of his life was to take some of the Rather children, my mother among them, to a circus. After seeing them home, he was stricken with apoplexy before reaching his own home and never regained consciousness. He left my grandfather his handsome watch and chain, which he had bought in Switzerland, and a set of old Paris china that is still prized by the family. He was very musical. His clarinet, with which he accompanied my grand-mother, lies today on her Chickering piano in the parlor. To the city of Tuscumbia he left the Deshler Female Institute as a memorial to his son, Brigadier General James Deshler. The building was splendidly located on one of the most attractive sites in the town, with a fine campus on which, among beautiful trees, was his own home, which was to be used as a residence for the head of the school. The institute flourished for many years but, sad to say, is no more, having been sacrificed in the name of progress.

The Rathers and the Warrens were dear friends and lived within a block of each other. There was a Warren child for every Rather child, even to twins. The children played together and were inseparable as young people. This close friendship between the two families (still cherished by their descendants) dates from the time my grandfather went to school to Mrs. Warren's father, "Old Parson Sloss," as Papá called him. The Reverend Mr. Sloss taught a private school and was the Presbyterian min-ister in Sommerville, Alabama, the little town that my great-grandfather helped to establish and named for his friend, Lieu-tenant Sommerville, who was killed at the Battle of New Orleans.

The Warren home in Tuscumbia was a charming old-fashioned house with peaked gables and dormer windows. The front portico, rose embowed, had long wide steps, and there on summer evenings the young people would gather and sing to the accompaniment of a guitar played by one of the Warren boys. Among the circle of friends at these gatherings were two young lawyers, Joseph E. Gilbert and James T. Kirk, who were part-ners. They never failed to be present at any gathering of the Warrens and the Rathers, and in due course, Joe married one of the Warrens and James married one of the Rathers—my mother.

All of the Warrens were musical, as was their beloved "Uncle William," who, when both Mr. and Mrs. Warren died at an early age, took the young family under his care. To me as a child he was a legendary figure, a man who was a native of Ireland and whom I had heard about but had never seen. But I can remember as a small child passing by the Warren house with my nurse on late afternoons and hearing the quavering notes of a violin, which I was told was the old man playing.

Miss Lucie Pettit and Cousin Ammie Keyes were among those who were contemporaries and girlhood friends of Mother and Tante and continued as regular visitors to Locust Hill even in my day. Both were beautiful women. Miss Lucie was the Dresden china type. She had many beaux, but something went awry with the real romance of her life, and she never married. After Cousin Ammie married and moved to Kentucky, she came less frequently.

When the Pettit family lost their fortune, Miss Lucie taught music and, as so often happened with Southern gentlewomen of those days, her frustrations withered her. Nevertheless, she was always sweet and lovely, though a bit wistful. The whole family was devoted to her, and she was the most loyal of friends. In the latter years of her life she seemed to cherish every memory connected with Locust Hill; and, when visiting here, she would gradually unfold in its loving, friendly atmosphere like those Japanese flowers that, when put in water, expand from little dried sticks into colorful blooms. She had developed many idiosyncrasies. She slept with her head to the north, which necessitated changing the position of her bed. She ate various health foods—a new one each summer. She held her little hands tightly clenched as if under great tension, but in time they would relax and unfold. Her trunks were the largest I ever saw and in them she carried a varied and prodigious amount of things. There were stacks of sheet music, newspapers saved from which the desired clippings were never cut, canceled checks, blankets, a mosquito net, a sadiron, a folding rack for drying clothes, and numerous "dress patterns" that she had acquired at sales during the winter. These she would generously distribute among friends whom she thought might need them. Early she acquired the habit of going with my grandmother and grandfather on their annual trip to Petoskey, Michigan, especially if Tante was going, too, and she continued going there every summer as long as she lived. After Tante married, she went with her and Uncle Weakley, or with Mother and Father and me; for we all followed Papá to Petoskey or some of those charming resorts around Little Traverse Bay.

The Years of My Childhood

RECENTLY I CAME UPON A FUGITIVE CLUSTER OF WHITE violets under the damson tree. It is one of the charms of old gardens that their flowers often go underground to reappear years later in unexpected spots. These pale blossoms set me dreaming of my childhood when my whole life was contained within the white picket fence that surrounded Locust Hill. "Beneath the trees I sat among the flowers, and with the flowers I played." No medieval tapestry was more flower-strewn than this lawn with its carpet of spring beauties, and the wild violets, clover, dandelions, Quaker ladies, and stars of Bethlehem that twinkled among them. Even now I delay the grass cutting until they have had their moment in the sun. Every nook and corner of the lawn was familiar to me, and whenever a flower, however early, opened an adventurous eye, I was the first to see it and take it to my mother, who preserved it between the pages of some book she was reading. I rarely open one of her old volumes without having a faded flower fall out. My best loved parts of the garden were the tangled, overgrown places, "the little lines of sportive wood run wild," where I felt far away and lost to view. For a child a too perfectly groomed garden lacks mystery and appeal; a garden, like poetry, should "surprise by a fine excess" and regale the senses with unexpected sweets. I always knew where the moss was greenest, the wood violets thickest, the places where the fairies had danced (a greener ring in the grasses told of their trespassing), the spot where four- and five-leaf clovers could be found. The five-leaf ones had to be given away at once or bad luck would come; the four-leaf had to be kept for good luck. All such haunts revive at the sight of dandelions, shiny brown acorn cups, bits of blue china, colored leaves, and the fairy tablecloths that spiders stretch upon the grass. My special duty as a child was to sweep these cobwebs from the box-wood hedges with a little broom that I had been given for that chore.

MARY WALLACE KIRK, AGE SIX

These recollected hours that have the charm
Of visionary things, those lovely forms
And sweet sensations that throw back our life
And almost make infancy
A visible scene, on which the sun is shining.

The years of my childhood seem to merge into one continuous whole, broken only by the different activities of summer and winter. Those warm summers seem always to have had blue skies filled with big, white clouds floating idly by. Of course there were days of rain and low-hung clouds, which made the earth so sodden you could almost see and smell the green things growing, when the wet bark of trees glistened and raindrops like crystals on the filaments of the cedars fell in showers upon me. But the shining, well-scrubbed morning face of the world always returned, and it was the sun-filled days that I loved most.

Is it so small a thing
To have enjoyed the sun?
To have lived light in the Spring?

My prints (when I was etching) were always so filled with sunlight that my instructor once asked with some impatience, "Doesn't it ever rain in Alabama?" His favorite themes were mines and subways and dark factories; my little cabins in a sun-filled landscape offended him.

I loved building playhouses among the moss green roots of trees, swinging high under the old paulownia tree, picking morning glory buds and turning them into ladies with purple velvet skirts, making clover chains, gathering "bunchkays" of flowers, or making mud pies and leaving them to dry in the sun with their icing of white sand. When my little friends came to see me, we played "hi-spy" among the shrubs and boxwood hedges or "fox in the morning" and other running games. Mother allowed us to rifle trunks of old clothes and parade around the garden in long black trains dragging doll carriages

SUNSET

THE WHIG ROSE

crammed with dolls. We fed them by "milking" (stripping) the tiny leaves from the fernlike mimosa foliage. At times I would try to go barefoot and to climb trees. My mother would come out and lend encouragement by giving me a boost up a tree, for she had loved such fun in her childhood. I took great joy in arranging boutonnieres for my father, grandfather, and uncles. Violets, old-fashioned pinks, a tiny rosebud, or a ragged robin were among their favorites.

When the Arkansas boys, John, Hal, Pearsall, and Gordon Rather, arrived, I had my air gun along with them. We became a band of hunters in the mornings and a baseball team in the afternoons. When the English sparrows grew such a nuisance that conversation on the porch afternoons and evenings was disturbed by their twitterings, my grandfather promised us ten cents a dozen for all we killed. One summer we made seventy-five cents. For convenience we carried the BB bullets in our mouths

THE ARKANSAS BOYS

and spit them into the hole at the top of the gun so as to be quick on the trigger. When we had a good "bag" we usually wanted them cooked; so heaping platters of them were served to us at dinner. No grownup partook of our kill. Our uncles, John D. and Courtenay, would come home early in the afternoons and make ready for the game of baseball. John D., the younger, or "Uncle" as he paid us to call him, was the pitcher, and Courtenay, the elder, who wanted to be called by his first name, was the catcher. Friends were invited to come and form a rival team. When the game was over, Mother served us ice cream and cake on the brick porch. When the Jones boys from New Jersey visited their relatives here, we were often invited to play in the big lane in front of the Johnsons' house where it widened out into a fine diamond. Miss Minnie, their aunt, always served the best peach ice cream in the world.

When I was five I was given a small plot of ground for a garden and a little rake and hoe and watering can. I gardened with enthusiasm. My specialty was Johnny-Jump-Ups, the "little western flower" or Love-in-idleness as Shakespeare calls it in *A Midsummer Night's Dream*. Of course I had to have a few of all the seeds that Mother ordered, and I was much addicted to cuttings. Strange how many of them lived! About this time the Hugh Stephenson family moved into the colonial cottage, and there were nine children, an abundance that seemed marvelous to my eyes. My garden bordered the fence that separated the two places, and the three youngest children, Susie, Annie, and Ned would climb up and sit on the fence and watch me work. In this way we got acquainted. Sometimes our mothers would come out and talk.

> I hear the neighbors say,
> talking across the fences about flowers
> My Duchess Rose is in full bloom;
> and have you seen my verbena?
> You must have a slip.
> A cheerful gossip good for childish ears.

Annie became my special friend, and we played together every day as long as the Stephensons lived in the cottage. One of our great joys was *Mother Goose*, and we knew much of it by heart. Sometimes Uncle would stand us up in front of him and examine us on it and give us picked-out pecan halves for correct answers.

When Mother had potted plants I had to have some too. Every tiny flower pot and empty tea tin I claimed for rooting cuttings and planting date seeds that usually produced little two- and three-frond palms. I had to have a green house or, rather, a pit. When we found a broken pane of glass Annie and I dug a hole, stuck flowers in it, and covered it with the glass. We finally decided to turn the garden into a nursery and transplanted dozens of little peach seedlings that we dug up from under one of the peach trees on the place. We called it the Kirk-Stephenson Nursery and made a catalogue out of yellow paper and illustrated it with colored crayons. The peach trees flourished and became a veritable thicket. They had to be thinned to four and eventually to one; from it the family ate peaches for many years.

Memories almost engulf me when I think of mornings on the porch. There would be years of them if they could be strung together—idyllic hours that held the stuff of gentle living. Each year from early summer until late September our mornings at home were spent on the porch. Here was leisure for companionship and for savoring the beauty of the day with its sights and sounds and fragrances—sunlight on wind-ruffled leaves; the mingled scent of boxwood and jasmine; the warm, prickly smell of cedar. Here was leisure for far ranging talk, when things of the past were handed down and related to things of the present. Continuity was here and a sense of security and belonging. Papá sat in his special chair, the one that had been his father's, and Mother sat beside him, a bit of needlework or a book in her lap, with Alp at their feet while I played nearby, listening to the good talk or sometimes being read to aloud.

Our porch extended across the west front of the house and

THE PORCH IN THE AFTERNOON

down the north side. In the mornings it was shady and there was always a breeze, especially at the corner where the swing hung. On the porch were a table, many chairs, cushions, a rug, magazines, and flowers—always flowers. Here house guests were entertained and callers that dropped in and spend-the-day guests who brought their fancy work. The habit of sitting on the porch in summer was a custom of long standing. In my mother's childhood her grandfather had been the center. He loved children and always had his pockets full of candy for them. The children would cluster around him to hear his stories and eat his candy. John D. and Mary Wallace, the twins, were his special favorites. And he considered a whipping much too severe even that time when they put sand in the buckets of fresh paint destined for the house.

At night on the porch with the men at home, there was much talk and laughter; but some nights my uncles would go calling, and then my mother, with me on her lap, my father, and my grandfather would be the only ones left. The trees, touched by the pale gleams from the lamps inside, looked like stage scenery, and the night would seem to cover us with a garment of stillness, fireflies embroidering the dark velvet of its folds. Then mother would sing to us the popular songs of her youth and some of the older ones that were my grandfather's favorites. I can remember always identifying myself with the people in the songs as well as with the locale—with "Jeanette," whose snood was always loosened that her lover might tangle his hand in her hair, and the "maiden, young and fair" that dwelt by "The Blue Alsatian Mountains." What a delighted thrill I finally had in actually seeing those mountains after so many years of distant acquaintanceship with them. There was another song whose title escapes me, but the first verses

> The sails are all swelling,
> The streamers float gay,
> The anchor is rising,
> And I must away.
> Adieu, my dear mountains; adieu, my
>   dear home

were just as poignant, though not so real, as when years later the old *Mauretania* with gay streamers flying slipped from her berth in New York, her band playing "Auld Lang Syne"—my mother and father and I on board. Among the favorites of my grandfather were "Normandy, My Normandy," "The Origin of the Harp," "The Last Rose of Summer," "Beautiful Venice, the Bride of the Sea," and "The Evening Gun." I liked the last one best, not sung on the porch but by my mother accompanying herself on the piano and striking the deep bass chords that were the gun. Hearing "Sweet Alice Ben Bolt," "Listen to the Mocking Bird," "I Dreamt I Dwelt in Marble Halls," "The Kerry Dancers," and "In the Gloaming," and many others was a wonderful way to drift off into sleep and to be carried upstairs to bed instead of having to be separated from the merry party and led off to bed after saying "Rosy dreams and slumbers light; to each and all a fair goodnight." I never wanted to go to bed; there were too many interesting things to see and to do and to hear. When absorbed in some play or project I remembered wondering how I would stand all those hours of darkness before I could play again.

I loved being with my young uncles, and they spent much time with me. They were very fond of playing chess and checkers. Some evenings they would go up to Courtenay's room for a game, and I would follow and watch them play until Mother or Father called me to come to bed. They always had refreshments on these evenings—one reason, I suppose, I liked to be there. They would toast marshmallows for me, and sometimes in the fall we would roast chestnuts or pop corn on the fire when the coals were glowing.

When Uncle dressed to go out calling, he liked for me to put the links in his cuffs and to hand him his gold collar buttons. He would set me upon the end of the dresser and tell me stories or talk to me while I carried out my assignment. One Sunday afternoon he told me that he was going to propose to a certain young lady I was devoted to, and he began to tell me what he was going to say to her. I cannot remember that part, but I do remember that in the midst of the practice proposal I burst into tears and was inconsolable. Whether what he said seemed too beautiful or whether I had some intimation that our relationship would change, I do not know. I only know that he took me in his arms and was a long time comforting me and assuring me that he was just pretending. When he told me a number of years later that he was to be married I even then shed a few tears. He built his house across the street from Locust Hill and visited us every day as did his wife, Nona, and his sons, Pratt and John D. IV. After his wife died and he was alone and I was alone, he had his meals with me until the time of his death.

Uncle was a very delightful person to be with and to hear

JOHN D. RATHER, JR.

talk. He seemed to attract interesting encounters and experiences. There is one of more than passing interest that occurred at the end of a vacation in 1918. He and his family had spent the summer in Sutton, Massachusetts, with his father-in-law. They had been driven into Worcester in time for lunch before leaving on the evening train. Uncle was very casual about carrying money with him, always thinking he could get a check cashed. But on this trip he had decided to take along an extra $100.00 bill to defray the incidental expenses en route home. When he took out his wallet to pay for the lunch in Worcester, he found only a $10.00 bill! "*Now*, what *are* you going to do?" his wife asked. "I am going to pick out the finest bank in the city and ask to have a check cashed."

When he entered the chosen bank, he went to the door marked *President* and told the uniformed page that he would like to see the president:

"Your card, Sir?"

"It is not necessary," Uncle replied.

He was admitted, and there at a desk sat an elderly gentleman with a face as stern and rugged as the granite of his New England hills.

"You do not know me," Uncle said. "My name is John D. Rather. I am a member of the law firm of Kirk and Rather, Tuscumbia, Alabama, and I have come to ask you to cash a check for $100.00 if I can convince you that I am an honest man."

"Have you any identification?"

"No, I have not; only my return ticket but that has no name on it."

"Why haven't you telegraphed for the money?"

"There is no Western Union office in my little town. Possibly you might question me on my section of the country, my profession, or some subject that would convince you that I am who I say I am."

"What town did you say you came from?"

"Tuscumbia, Alabama."

"Is there anything outstanding about that community?"

"It is the birthplace of Helen Keller of whom you have doubtless heard."

"I meant something in the way of a natural phenomenon?"

"We have a Big Spring, one of the largest in the United States. Its daily output at this time has been estimated as sufficient to give every person in the country four gallons of water a day."

"On what railroad is your town located?"

"The Southern Railway, Memphis Division. Its the halfway point between Chattanooga and Memphis."

"Name the town immediately west of your city."

Here Uncle was Macgregor on his native heath. Papá having been president of the railroad, Uncle had known, even as a child, every station in geographical order from Chattanooga to Memphis. As he named a town the old gentleman would say, "The next?" "The next?" "The next?" until Corinth was named:

"Anything outstanding in that place?"

"I suppose you refer to the Battle of Shiloh." As Uncle gave the names of the commanding generals on both sides, he saw a faint smile creep over the old gentleman's face as he said, "After that battle, as captain of a company, I was ordered by forced march to overtake some of the Confederate forces, and late in the afternoon, footsore and weary, we stopped on the banks of the Big Spring in Tuscumbia to refresh ourselves. It was the best water I ever drank, and from that day to this I have never met anyone who had so much as heard of the place. How much money did you say you wanted?"

Always fascinated by machinery, Uncle kept a small stationary engine, a relic of his *Youth's Companion* days, on a little table in his room, and I loved to watch him run it. And there was nothing he liked better than mending things, clocks in particular. After a trying term of court, he found relaxation in taking an old clock to pieces, mending it, and putting it together again. His friends never let him be without one for such a purpose. As a little boy he had said he wanted to be "a man what fixes clocks." He loved games and taught me how to play caroms, checkers, bagatelle, and parcheesi. He made a set of "Authors" cards by hand, and Charlotte Jackson, one of my little friends, and I played with them until we wore them out, but not before we knew every quotation by heart and the name of its author.

Fresh from the University, Uncle read law in Father's office, and they became law partners. He was very much in demand as a public speaker for historical occasions, Memorial Day celebrations, Lee's birthday, Fourth of July, school commencements, and political gatherings. I was always his audience when he was memorizing a speech. I can still quote passages from them and from poems that he used.

Uncle and Courtenay always went together to cut and bring in the tree at Christmas. I remember that the first time I went with them I was secretly in tears over the smallness of the tree they chose because I wanted a big tree, but when it was mounted and placed in the parlor it touched the ceiling! After the tree was in place, the smell of cedar and the feel of secret preparations pervaded the house. And there was the hurry and bustle of putting up the evergreens, decorating the tree, going on last minute errands, meeting the trains for home coming relatives. An ardent letter writer, I wrote numerous letters to Santa Claus, in whom I believed implicitly, and it thrilled me to watch them swirl up the chimney, which was my method of mailing them. I even imagined I could hear his reindeer on the roof, and one Christmas I insisted on giving him a pair of gloves and left them by the fireplace for him.

On Christmas Eve, about the middle of the afternoon, I was dressed up with a spray of holly or mistletoe pinned on my coat and sent out in the carriage to deliver the gaily wrapped gifts to the homes of our friends and to wish them "Merry Christmas." I would return with almost as many packages as I had started out with!

Christmas morning began with the exciting game of catch-

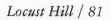

COURTENAY RATHER

PEARSALL RATHER

ing all and sundry "Christmas gift." This custom, no doubt, had its origin in before-the-war days when all the servants would come to the big house on Christmas morning saying, "Christmas gift? Christmas gift?" and their presents would be given to them. No longer did those words imply an obligation, only the fun of catching someone or being caught. This custom necessitated early rising, much tiptoeing, dodging around corners, hiding behind doors in order to surprise the unwary; since the words were on everyone's tongue, it was often difficult to decide who was the winner. "I said it first," would be challenged by "No, I said it first because I said it loudest," or "I finished saying it before you did." It was the height of my ambition to have a better score than my uncles. In the end everyone on the place was involved; even if the telephone rang you said "Christmas gift" before saying "Hello."

Before breakfast came the opening of the stockings that hung across the mantel in the library, Papá's special room. No other activity or Christmas custom, even the tree, ever had the same aura or so held in essence that indefinable Christmas feeling. Breakfast was always especially good, with, possibly, spareribs, hominy grits, eggs any style, hot biscuits, waffles, syrup, preserves, and of course coffee and tea.

Later in the morning we gathered around the lighted tree, family, guests, and servants; Uncle having been chosen to distribute the gifts, he carried out his assignment with many amusing comments and guesses as to what the packages contained. There was much laughter and delight expressed over the gifts. Such joy and excitement continued into the afternoon when the big turkey dinner was announced. All of us who were children vied with each other to see who could eat the most. At night a beautiful display of fireworks was presented by Courtenay and Uncle.

One Christmas a terrible thing happened. Uncle was very particular about the Christmas presents he gave to the young ladies that were his friends. He kept an even balance between two here in Tuscumbia. On this special Christmas he was giving one a locket and the other a pin, and he asked Tante, who with Uncle Weakley was spending the holidays with us, to gift-wrap them for him; he asked Uncle Weakley to deliver them on Christmas morning (we were still in the horse-and-buggy days). Uncle had an engagement with Miss Ella for Christmas night and with Miss Annie for the night after. When he arrived at Miss Ella's home, she met him wearing the locket and began to thank him for it. "But that is not the present I sent you," he explained, whereupon he took the locket and declared he would be back in a short while. There was a kind of suppressed excitement when Uncle returned home and called out Tante and Uncle Weakley for what seemed a kind of mysterious conference. Uncle Weakley hurried away, and Uncle remained. After some time Uncle Weakley returned, and Uncle left. Then the mystery cleared. In delivering the presents Uncle Weakley had gotten them mixed up; so it became his embarrassing duty to go to Miss Annie, explain, get the pin, and deliver the locket. That the pin was a little prettier than the locket added to the embarrassment.

Courtenay was more reserved about the young ladies he called on than Uncle and loved to keep us guessing as to where he was going on the nights when he went calling. When he came down to dinner dressed for the occasion, we knew he would be going to see one of the two young ladies that he especially liked, but for all of our questioning, Papá joining in, he would give no clue. One of them lived in the extreme west end of town and the other in the extreme east end. At that time there was no electricity or street lights in the community; so Courtenay always took a lantern for the long walk. As he left, I would run upstairs to watch for the lantern from the windows and in that way be able to report to the family the direction in which he was going. I had to watch the light for some minutes or he would fool me by starting in one direction then changing to the other. Whenever the Arkansas boys came, Courtenay was the one who took us fishing, blackberrying, and on mountain trips. He was always asking riddles and telling funny stories. He built a play house for us big enough for all to get in and play "keeping house." We loved it, especially when it rained; it seemed so cozy and shut in.

Another of our special delights was mashing pins. We accumulated pins of all kinds and sizes for making scissors and pieces of wire to make our initials; we collected nails for swords and spears. The pieces of wire we also twisted into various shapes, vying with each other for new ideas. Hal was the most original in his finds and in his experiments. When train time approached, some member of the family went with us to the railroad track, for we never were allowed to go alone. We then set to work, each in his special preserve along the track, and laid out our collections, using spit to make them stick. It took a great deal of that commodity, and one's supply sometimes gave out. Hal often called to his older brother, "John, come lend me some spit." Mashing pins was a precarious enterprise beset with many hazards, such as the jarring of the rails by a heavy engine or the number of coaches that had to pass. A long freight train could be disastrous, and often we found our treasures broken and scattered. To boast a perfect pair of scissors or a perfect spear was to be envied. We were avid for little pasteboard boxes in which to keep our collections, the mashed and the unmashed, and commandeered all available ones.

Pearsall in addition had a tin box in which he kept bees, for he could catch them without being stung. This ability gave him great distinction. But woe to the rest of us if we opened that tin box! We had bottles with tadpoles, collected on fishing trips, which we longingly examined each day, hoping to see them turn into frogs. That they never did, at least not while in our possession. Once we imprisoned a caterpillar expecting to see a butterfly come forth. And we made lanterns by catching fireflies and putting them in bottles. How vile our hands would smell! Fireflies never came out before dusk; so our hands had to have a severe scrubbing before the evening meal.

One day Mary and Fanny told Mother they were to be married in a double wedding. It was to be at night in the First Baptist Church, the one to which they belonged. When the time came, Mother arranged their veils and their bouquets, and all of us went to the wedding. For decorations there were two arches entwined with vines and flowers, and each couple stood under an arch. The ceremony was performed by the Reverend Wilson Northcross, a famous Baptist minister of the community, who is said to have baptized in the Big Spring more than 3,000 souls. The wedding was truly a double one, for he first married Bud Keller to Fanny Waddell and then married Simon Floyd to Mary Walker; then he married Fanny to Bud and Mary to Simon.

I was so deeply impressed by the wedding, the first I had seen, that I immediately wanted to have a similar one for my dolls. That summer two cousins, Annie and Elizabeth Baker from Rose Hill, came to visit us, and I inspired them with my enthusiasm. My dolls and Elizabeth's (Annie was much older) were to be the principals; so we set to work to make trousseaux for them. We pressed Annie into service and sewed almost to exhaustion. Elizabeth would become so frustrated over her sewing difficulties that at intervals she would throw down her work and say, "I am not going to let her marry!" That would be a heavy blow, for we had planned a *double* wedding. Finally with Mother's help the brides and grooms were suitably dressed. The brides had dresses with trains and veils, and there were suits for traveling and a "second day's" dress such as Mary and Fanny had had as well as other clothes. I was going to take the dolls with us to Bay View for their wedding trip, and Elizabeth's were to have the trip home with her.

The night before the cousins left, the wedding took place on top of the big square piano in the parlor. Mother had decorated it and arranged a tableau wedding with a doll audience seated in proper order. The two couples stood under croquet wickets that she had entwined with vines and flowers. Uncle performed the ceremony and all the family, along with the two cousins who lived across the street, assembled in the parlor to witness it. I had a little suitcase in which I carried the bride and groom and trousseau to Bay View. Each day I changed the bride's costume and like all brides and grooms they attracted much attention and became favorites among the guests at the hotel.

I was much given to planning evening entertainments, for I hoped to avoid going to bed as long as possible. During the day I would write out programs and at dinner time put one at each person's plate. Recently I came upon one of them in my sprawling handwriting and with atrocious spelling. I had arranged for a solo by Mrs. James T. Kirk, a duet by Miss Bessie Rather and Miss Letitia Rather (my young lady cousins who lived across the

ON BAPTIST HILL

street), and speeches by Mr. James T. Kirk, Mr. John D. Rather, and Mr. Courtenay Rather. Halfway down the program was "Conversation by Everybody." I knew what was inevitable and so provided for it. Recitation by Miss Mary Wallace Kirk and a Magic Lantern Show by Mr. John D. Rather completed the program. Written across the back of the program was "Come Interested."

The Magic Lantern, precursor of the home-shown travel slides of today, was one of my great delights as was also the Scroll of Bible Pictures illustrating the fascinating Old Testament stories. These latter made such an impression on me that when I saw Father looking over the wreckage of a tray of dishes dropped by the maid I accused him of looking like Nehemiah contemplating the ruins of Jerusalem. Another favorite was the stereoscope with its mysterious two pictures that you saw as one. It was always in demand during an illness. I could imagine myself in the places I saw and forget how I felt. When I was convalescing Mother always spread the "crazy quilt" over my bed—a fascinating assortment of dress samples from family and friends put together with fancy stitches. The velvet and satin pieces often had flowers or scenes painted on them. Each piece had its associations.

Almost every year Ringling Brothers Circus would come to Florence just five miles away. Tante lived there, and great was the excitement when circus day arrived. An early breakfast was necessary if we were to be on time for the parade. We had to go in the carriage, and Papá did not approve of fast driving; in fact, part of the ritual of any trip to Florence saw the men getting out and walking up the steep hill that led into the town in order to spare the horses.

From Tante's porch we watched the parade of elephants and camels with their bespangled riders, prancing horses beautifully caparisoned, giraffes, zebras, lions, tigers, and a rhinoceros, all in red and gold cages, and an old hippopotamus lolling in his bath. Mr. Ringling himself would pass by in a shiny Victoria, and near the end would be the gaudy snake charmer fondling her necklace of snakes, a cage of monkeys followed by clowns, and finally the calliope with its weird, plaintive music.

After a hurried lunch we would be off to the circus grounds with the big tents, flying pennants, side shows and barkers, vendors of peanuts, popcorn, balloons, cotton candy, and pink lemonade. In and over all would be that unforgettable smell of wild animals, fried foods, trampled grass, and sawdust. We never went into the side shows but made straight for the animal tent, which was Papá's special interest. To me the bareback riders and the trapeze performers furnished the thrills.

Bicycles had come into great popularity about this time, and a Florence school friend of Uncle's who could do all manner of stunts on one joined Ringling Brothers' Circus and became the man who did the loop of death on a bicycle in a glass globe. He married one of the bareback riders, the aristocrats of the circus, and years later Uncle and Tante, at different times, saw him perform. Uncle went behind the scenes and visited with him. Finally he met his death in his act.

During my early years Mother was constantly my playmate. She invented games and helped me furnish my indoor doll house that Courtenay had made for me. It had four rooms, was two stories high with chimneys, and had fireplaces with mantels and a stairway. From Little Rock Uncle Hal sent me the most adorable set of parlor furniture with sofa and chairs upholstered in wine-colored velvet and a marble top table. Every room was completely furnished. I had a beautiful miniature dinner service that had belonged to my little Aunt Mary Wallace and pieces of a tea set that had been Mother's. Mother made the curtains and rugs, sheets and bedspreads, tablecloths and napkins, some embroidered or hemstitched. I helped make them, for I was taught early to sew a fine seam. Uncle made the dining room furniture, carving it out of cigar boxes—a really charming sideboard complete with mirror and drawers that opened and shut, a table, and gilded highback dining room chairs of attractive design.

Best of all I loved to be read to by Mother. She read aloud so beautifully and made her stories so vivid that long after I could read myself I imposed upon her. "Wynken, Blynken, and Nod" was one of my early favorites, as were the "Rock-a-bye Lady" from "Hush-a-bye Street," "Little Boy Blue" and other Eugene Field characters, as well as James Whitcomb Riley's irrepressible children. "Uncle Remus" held me enthralled as completely as he did the "Little Boy." "Diddie, Dumps, and Tot" was a great favorite as were the "Little Colonel" books, "Melody," and "Captain January," "Little John Fauntleroy," and "Sarah Crew," Foster's "Story of the Bible," and many others. I loved to hear Mother read Jean Ingelow's "High Tide on the Coast of Lincolnshire":

> Cusha! Cusha! Cusha! calling,
> For the dews will soon be falling;
> Leave your meadow grasses mellow,
>   mellow, mellow;
> Quit your cowslips, cowslips yellow;
> Come uppe Whitefoot, come uppe Lightfoot;
>
>   . . .
>
> Come uppe Jetty, rise and follow,
> Jetty, to the milking shed.

Always learning poetry by heart, I memorized on my seventh birthday Jean Ingelow's "Seven Times One." Longfellow and Tennyson soon became my favorite poets. One evening Father was reading "Enoch Arden" to me and when he reached the part where Enoch returns and through the window sees his wife and children in a happy family group with another man I burst into tears and cried so bitterly that Father had to stop reading and comfort me. It was years before I could bring myself to read the poem to the end.

Mother showed me how to draw and paint and how to make all manner of Christmas and birthday presents for members of the family, such as pen wipers of green felt, cut in the shape of lily pads, each with a turtle sitting on top. The turtle was made of half an English walnut shell, his protruding head and feet cut from black paper. I made blotters decorated with groups of mice—apple seeds run through with black darning cotton snipped off short for the nose but long for the tail. We made heart-shaped needle books of velvet and the most attractive little velvet watch cases for father and my uncles to put their watches in when they were taken off at night. To lay them on a cold marble top dresser would cause the mainspring to snap.

On our rides in the country we were always on the lookout for passion flowers when in season and the lovely balls on the sweetgum and sycamore trees and for the good little fox grapes that came in the autumn and chestnuts and summac leaves. From the fruit of the passion flower Mother would cut little baskets with handles and pinked edges, and I filled them with tiny flowers. In the wide open blossoms she showed me the cross that gave the flower its name, and the buds she turned into Fiji Islanders with big hats and gaily fringed cloaks.

TENANT HOUSE,
KIRKFIELD FARM

JAMES T. KIRK

These country rides were usually out to our farm, Kirkfield, Father's special delight, as it is mine today. Mother often said that he practiced law to support the farm.

Father was a very studious person, quiet and gentle, with very high standards of character and conduct, and he loved the study of law. He practiced for sixty years, and I often heard him say that he had never grown tired of it. Judges of our Alabama Supreme Court have spoken to me of the fine quality of his briefs. Very public spirited, he was always in the forefront of any enterprise for the betterment of the community, a man who in his thinking was ahead of his time. People today mention that fact to me. Education was another interest, and no young man ever came to him for help in getting an education who was not given assistance. But his hobby was his farm—Kirkfield.

He had great dreams for it and was always eager to bring his tenants up to a higher standard of living and of agricultural practices. In so doing, he tried many experiments. One, I remember, involved a tenant named Jim to whom he had assigned a small acreage; Father was to furnish all the mules, the equipment, and other necessary supplies. One day that spring Jim sent word that one of the mules had died. Father had another sent out immediately. Two days later a message was received that another mule had died. Being engaged in court, Father could not go out but ordered a replacement. When news came of the death of the third mule, he and Mother and I went out to the farm on Sunday afternoon. When we drove up to Jim's house and asked to see him, his wife said that he had gone to the crossroads. Father explained that he had come to see about the death of the mules. "Yes," she said, "that's what's taken Jim to the cross-roads. He's mightily pestered about the death of them mules, but I told Jim he oughtn't to be so pestered for the Father, He taken them mules." As we rode away Mother said that she had heard of many things laid on the Lord but this was the first time she had heard Him accused of taking mules.

Mother often played lady-come-to-see with me and has told

me that once when playing the game I, as usual, was the hostess entertaining her. We were seated at a little table set up with a doll tea set with tea cakes and water for tea. She was in lively conversation with me about my family of dolls when I slipped down from my chair and whispered in her ear, "Mother, you are doing too much," then resumed my seat as if nothing had happened. She felt quite rebuked, she said, for overacting the part and began talking about more realistic things.

Nothing played a more prominent part in my childhood or was more beloved than my red shawl. Any ordinary definition of a shawl is wholly inadequate for understanding what that garment meant to me. It stood for warmth, for pleasure, for independence, for solitude in faraway places. It was a kind of magic carpet for dreams as well as a symbol of the absolute security of home. My mother would take me bundled up in the red shawl for a frolic in the snow, a rare and glorious occasion. We would run, loving to feel the snow in our faces, and play snowball and laugh with glee and bring in snow for a big bowl of snowcream. When we came in she would read me snow poems. I remember best Lowell's "The First Snowfall," which I learned by heart. A snow was always a signal for the preparation of some special food like crullers or muffin cakes or candy. And there was a favored menu—scalloped oysters served with hot chocolate and whipped cream. This was a great favorite with Uncle, and he often asked for it saying, "When you whip the cream, just wear it out." We would always put out food for the birds and then take our seats at the window and watch the little fluffed-up fellows fly down to eat while we chanted:

> The North wind doth blow
> And we shall have snow
> And what will the robin do then, poor thing?
> He will sit in the barn
> And keep himself warm,
> And hide his head under his wing, poor thing.

SNOW AT LOCUST HILL

Wrapped in my red shawl, I made that first trip alone across the garden to my grandmother's. Equipped with a candle, pencil and tablet, and the red shawl, I would seek the solitude of the closed-off stairway; halfway up was my favorite spot and the one most frequented by the muses. The red shawl made a wonderful tent stretched over four chairs with tall backs of equal height where I could crawl in and lie down in blissful discomfort. When I was sick, the comfort of comforts was to be rocked to sleep in Mother's lap with the red shawl over me while she sang to me. "Nellie Gray," was a favorite, especially that part about "the low green valley on the old Kentucky shore where I whiled many happy hours away." If Mother continued singing the rest of the song I would bring her back by saying, "Low green valley, low green valley." Somehow to feel myself in such a lovely spot as I pictured that to be helped the sick feeling. The "green pastures and still waters" of the twenty-third psalm gave me the same feeling. I liked, too, "What are the wild waves saying, Sister, the whole day long?" That song was about a little sick boy whose sister had taken him to the seashore.

At an early age I was given a little desk and bookcase combined that was a source of great joy and pride because on those shelves I could keep the books that were really mine. Another loved activity was the collecting of pictures to make scrapbooks. The wonderful advertisements in the magazines of today with their gorgeous pictures make me long to have had them when a child. How I would have gloated over them! Making a scrapbook was a favorite rainy day activity, as was the writing of the "Rainy Day News" or "The Evening Echo." Recently I came upon a copy of each. The sheets of paper were lined off into columns, and news of the family's doings recorded under appropriate headings. National and international events were mentioned but dealt with rather summarily. These papers were given to my father and uncles when they came home in the evenings. One evening to my awed astonishment they told me of a gentleman from Chicago who had called at the office that afternoon and inquired where he could get in touch with Miss Mary Wallace Kirk, from whom he had had a letter making inquiry about a set of books. He had come to show them and to sell them to her. I became limp at the enormity of what I had done. Having seen an advertisement for "The World's Best Poetry" in ten volumes which said that a booklet with a selection of the poems would be sent on the receipt of ten cents, I had, on my own, written for the booklet and enclosed a dime from my twenty-five cent weekly allowance. But my suspense was soon relieved, for Father had been so pleased at my venture that he had bought the books for me. Of course, they became my prized possession for many years and are still in use. Later I was a great collector of Perry Pictures and spent most of my allowance for those reproductions of the masterpieces of painting, sculpture, and architecture, which could be bought for a few cents each. Madonnas were my specialty, and my favorites among them were the Madonna Granduca and the Madonna of the Chair, and the Winged Victory of Samothrace among the statues.

I am very glad that I grew up before hammocks went out of style. A hammock was as much a part of summer equipment as the croquet set, the ping-pong table, and the tennis court.

Once Courtenay made a hammock of barrel staves, but it was not a success. You had to learn the technique of "staying put," which was complete immobility, for at the slightest movement it would turn upside down. I liked the soft woven ones with fringe along the sides, the kind you could sink down in. I can remember long summer afternoons when I would lie in the hammock reading the Alcott books or just dreaming as I watched the cloud shadows on the hills and the crisp yellow boxelder leaves falling on the grass; the faraway shine of a late August sun gave me the feeling of sadness that comes with summer's end.

It was always such fun when Father and the uncles came in at one o'clock for lunch. I was hugged and kissed and often went to the table on the shoulder of one of them. The household took on new life and interest. It was the same when they returned in the evening. If it was winter, the rooms were freshened up, the debris of the day put away, and the fires made to glow. In summer there was a similar routine in keeping with the season. The men brought the news of the day and gave accounts of any interesting people they had seen, just as Mother did when she had been calling or shopping:

> If she goes out to make a call,
> Or out to take a walk,
> We leave our work when she returns,
> And run to hear her talk.

If court was in session there would be much talk of law, for all the men, my grandfather included, were lawyers. Mother and I would sit quietly by. Sometimes she would put in a woman's opinion that usually cut through the maze of abstractions and offered a practical solution. Once, after an involved discussion, I amused them by asking, "You have to twist the law sometimes, don't you?" Mother loved politics and always took an active and usually a partisan part in political discussions. The members of my family were rarely on the popular side of a political question. My grandfather had opposed secession. He thought that slavery was wrong and that the issue could have been settled by negotiation, though when the issue was decided he went with his state. During the great free silver debate, all of the family were "sound money" democrats, not followers of Bryan.

At the table funny stories of happenings in court were often told, for Southern people have a great storytelling tradition. I remember one about a lawsuit involving the digging of a well in which a mule was to be given in payment. Old Tom, Ghee's brother, was a "well witcher," and he had "witched the well." When he was put on the stand for his testimony he declared, "All I know 'bout it is that the well-digger, he dug, and he dug, and he dug 'til he dug up the mule."

Summer was the great time for guests—the regulars and the irregulars. Uncle George and his daughters always came, sometimes together, sometimes separately. Uncle George often brought a friend with him. Cousin Jesse and Cousin Fannie were accomplished musicians and, when they came, there would be musical evenings with friends invited in. The summer that Cousin Jesse's fiancé came to meet the family I thought very exciting; for to me, a child, nothing was more alluring than a couple in love. Cousin Jesse's children and grandchildren continue to come to Locust Hill from as far away as Dallas, Texas.

Uncle Silas and his daughter, Augusta, were regulars. Augusta was full of fun and devoted to Mother. After her father's death, she lived with us for more than a year. Later she became a nurse and was with the Japanese bacteriologist, Dr. Hideyo Noguchi, in Quito, Ecuador, when he discovered the yellow fever parasite. Although she married and lived in California, she continued to come on visits here as long as she lived and always called Locust Hill home. Of course, the Arkansas boys were here and often Uncle Hal or Aunt Lila would bring them or come for them. To accommodate all these returning uncles, aunts, and cousins, the dining room table would be stretched its full length. If there were more than fourteen, a side table was set up for us children; otherwise we sat with the grownups and took part in the conversation, but by no means monopolized it. Papá sat at the foot of the table and did the carving. There was decorum and order wherever he presided, whether in the State Senate when he was thirty-six years old and its president or at his own table when he was eighty. He enjoyed good conversation as well as good food, and his table was amply provided with both; Mother catered to the appetites of her family and guests, always remembering their favorite dishes, nor did she forget the children.

Those of us who were children then always love to recall the amusing incidents of those days. "Don't you remember when Hal asked Uncle George's pompous friend, by whom he was sitting, 'Mr. Jones, do you like jelly?' 'Yes, Hal, I'm very fond of jelly.' 'Punch him in the belly.' " And one night when hearing a disturbance in the kitchen, Mother asked Safronia, one of the maids, what had happened. With complete aplomb she replied, "My brother has just fallen into the cistern."

My grandfather was an excellent raconteur and public speaker and could tell an anecdote with rare wit and charm. Having taken note of how everyone laughed and enjoyed his good stories, I one day tried to tell what I thought was a funny story. As I piled detail upon detail my grandfather at intervals would say, "Come to the point, come to the point, my daughter; get on with the story. Not so much detail." Alas, the story was never finished, for I left the table in tears, and it was a long time before I made another such attempt. When I did the point was quite to the fore. My next attempt to improve my conversational ability was equally unsuccessful. I listened carefully to an incident told by my mother that was received with great merriment. I had it letter perfect and when away from the family and on my own I told it. It elicited not so much as a smile or a comment. It was then I realized that it is not so much the content of a story that matters as the personality and charm of the teller.

My young uncles loved to tease, and my grandfather and I were their special targets. He more than knew how to take care of himself and turn the tables on them, but I did not and would often have to leave the table because of the flow of tears. Neither my father nor my mother ever intervened or came to my rescue. They thought, I discovered in later years, that I should learn to take care of myself, even this hard way. But whenever the uncles went too far Papá would reprimand them. I loved them so much that to hear them corrected was equally distressing, and I would

WHERE FANNY LIVED

say, with tears running down my cheeks, "Papá, I don't mind it," and we would all be happy again.

Happiness has been an essential part of my concept of life both for myself and for those around me, if I could bring it to pass. I am told that when I was three years old I asked my Uncle Pearsall, "What is emotion?" When he told me it was something you feel, I said, "Then happiness is an emotion for I feel happy." And so I might almost say with Wordsworth:

> My whole life I have lived in pleasant thought,
> As if life's business were a summer mood;
> As if all needful things would come unsought
> To genial faith.

One evening just before dinner, company came in unexpectedly, and the cook needed more eggs to augment the menu in some way. She asked me to get them for her. These old houses built in the 1820's and thereabouts are noted for not having any closets. Ours boasted only one, known as the "dark closet," located under the stairway and reached by a door in a recess of the library, the room where family and guests were assembled. Here were kept the sugar bucket, the extra supply of coffee, tea, and eggs. There is no greater fallacy than the supposition that children are not embarrassed by such errands. I was miserable at the thought of appearing before the guests with an armful of eggs. Only family pride and a fair habit of obedience enabled me to undertake the errand. Slowly and with feigned casualness I wandered around the room to the closet door, entered, and gently pulled the door almost to, leaving a faint line of light around its edges. This was the only illumination in the closet. As I tiptoed to reach the basket of eggs in the semidarkness, I had a sudden inspiration. I had on a little plaid skirt with a red sailor blouse. Why not put the eggs in my blouse? I could then walk freely before the guests, and no one would know that I was harboring eggs. Carefully I began putting them in it. They grew a little heavy, and my blouse sagged in places, but I had been told the number to bring, so I continued. As I put in the last egg, it slipped from my fingers. I heard a dreaded sound and with horror saw a yellow stream of egg issuing from my blouse and running down my skirt. Judging from the amount, all the eggs must have been broken. Tears began to flow in equal quantity. There, alone, in the "dark closet" I spent the most dejected minutes of my life. I would not leave; I would not call for help. My possible discovery seemed as horrible to contemplate as my immediate predicament.

At length my mother became concerned over the lateness of the meal and went to the kitchen to investigate. There a frantic cook told her that she had sent me for the eggs and that I had not returned. I have always appreciated my mother's deep understanding of the situation and of my feelings, but I marvel at how she controlled her keen and spontaneous sense of humor when she opened the door and was confronted with her dejected, egg-covered, tear-stained child. To her suggestion that I come with her and change my dress I dramatically refused. She did not urge me but gathered up the required number of eggs and returned to the closet with sufficient equipment to make me presentable. We emerged serene and fresh from the crowded darkness and to my infinite relief neither family nor guests seemed to be aware that catastrophe, mortification, and despair had been present immediately behind their backs. It never occurred to me that they had been told about it and also how to comport themselves.

One winter Mother had been called out of town on account of illness in Uncle Hal's family. Papá was convalescing after an attack of grippe, and I was given the responsibility of taking his tonic to him each morning. It was a very disagreeable dose that he thoroughly disliked. In fact, he did not approve of taking much medicine and had said to the doctor: "I do not want you to make an apothecary shop of my stomach." One day when I took him the dose as he sat by the south library window reading, he refused to take it. I continued to stand beside him holding the glass. Finally he looked up and said, "You are a persistent little piece." "Just a chip off the old block, Papá." He chuckled, reached for the glass, and drank the medicine.

Before Mother returned, General Charles Shelley, a friend of Papá's, came to see him. I was quite excited, for I was sitting at my mother's place at the table, and I was going to have to do the honors. Accordingly, I felt very proud when at breakfast from behind the silver service I asked, "General Shelley, will you have coffee or tea? Sugar and cream?" I remember the dress Fanny put on me for dinner that night. It was a red cashmir and over it she had put my prettiest pinafore, which was made of dimity with ruffles over the shoulders edged with lovely lace. After dinner I sat in the library with the gentlemen until my bed time, and I remember hearing General Shelley tell of a friend of his and Papá's who had been minister to Spain and while there was one of those appointed to witness the birth of the royal heir, this being a custom of the Spanish court at that time. The child who was born became Alfonso XIII. General Shelley said that the little naked baby was shown to the witnesses on a silver salver. That story created a vivid picture in my mind that I have never forgotten. The next day the General presented me with the first large, grown-up box of candy I ever had; so of course I remember him fondly and his gift to the "hostess."

I remember vividly the first play I was taken to see. Mother was determined that in introducing me to the world of the theater the first actor I saw should be a fine one, not one from the inferior traveling companies that came to our little Opera House, as it was called. When she was growing up, Papá always had taken her and Tante to Memphis, for that was the nearest city with the best attractions. And I can remember hearing her tell about seeing Booth and Barrett in Shakespearean roles and about hearing Materna sing. When Richard Mansfield came to Birmingham in *The Student Prince*, she took me to see him.

I shall never forget the sensation I had when the door of the theater opened and I stepped inside onto the carpet—truly a magic one. I was transported into a world that seemed filled with new and strange music, for I had never before heard an orchestra; even now when I go to the theater I miss the mood that it engendered. The tempered lighting, the gilded ornamentation of the building, the dressed-up men and women all contributed to the inner excitement and anticipation with which I watched for the great curtain to go up. Then came the foreign looking stage sets and the handsome prince who dominated the scene. Ever after, Richard Mansfield was my ideal of how a prince should look and act. And I was always thrilled when I came across his picture in some magazine.

Sister Julia lived across the street from us on the corner in an old-fashioned storey-and-a-half house with a long, sloping roof and a porch across the front, partially enclosed by lattice, and there were circles of boxwood in the yard. It had been her home when she was a girl. She was the widow of Mother's older brother, Eldon, and I called her Sister Julia because Mother did. She dearly loved children and was always ready to play with me. She taught me to knit, to shirr, to roll-and-whip, and when I was a little older, to make rolls. Her two daughters, Bessie and Letitia, gifted in doing needle work, made doll dresses for me.

But what Sister Julia and I loved best to do was to play logomachy. I remember one winter there was a big snow that stayed a long time. She would send Vic, her maid, for me, and bundled up in the red shawl I would go over and spend the day with her playing logomachy. Vic served our midday meal in the living room in front of the fire, and I thought that was wonderful. I can see her now bringing in covered dishes of steaming rice and black-eyed peas, and we made hoppin'-John. And how good it tasted! Sister Julia and I both loved rice inordinately; another taste we had in common was crackers, plain "soda crackers" as they then were called. She would have Pris, her little maid, Vic's daughter, bring in a bowl of them and place them so that we could reach over while playing and take one. The object of logomachy was to teach a child how to spell, but with me it

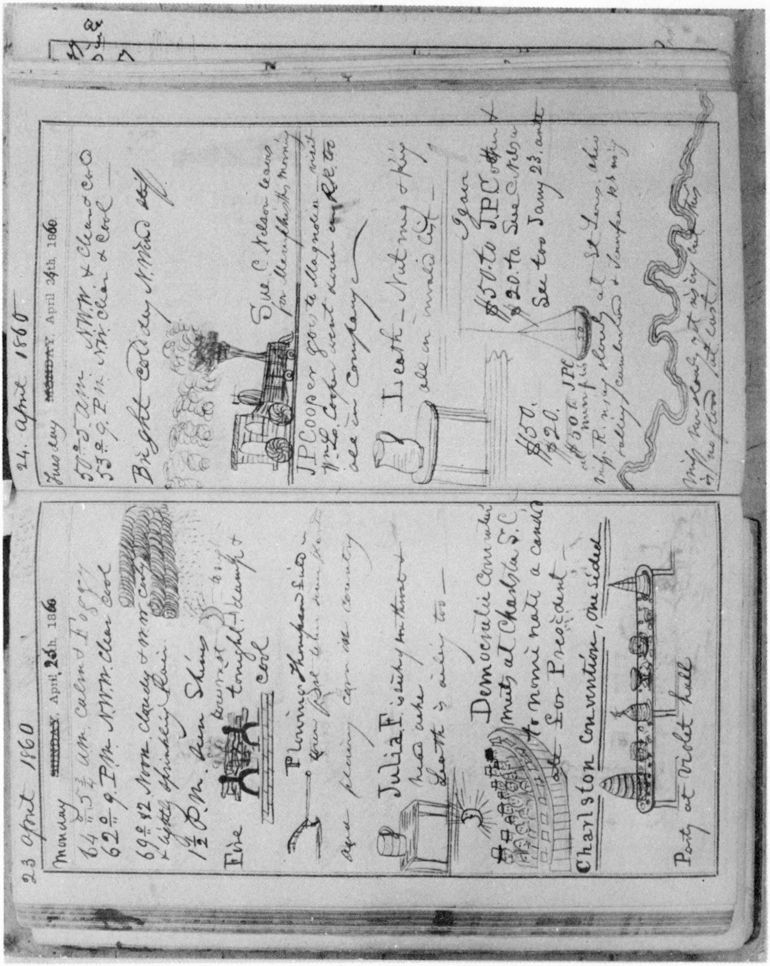

PAGES FROM WILLIAM COOPER'S DIARY

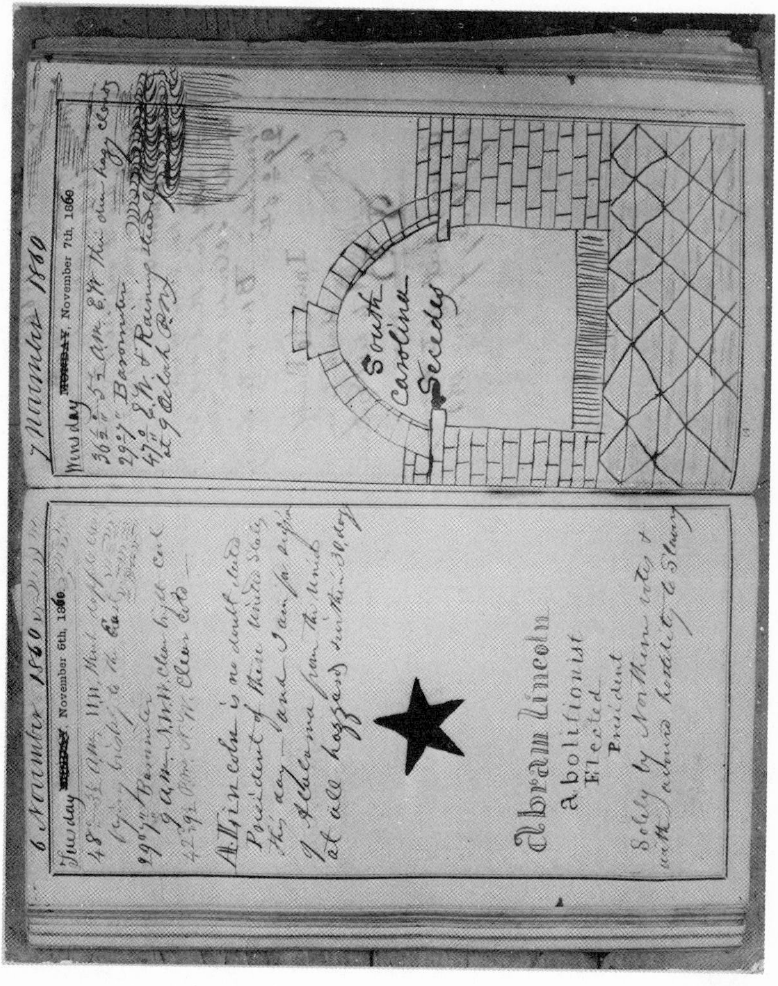

6 November 1860

Tuesday November 6th 1860

48° 3½ A.M. W.N. Wind [illegible]
[illegible]
29½° Barometer
9 A.M. N.N.W. Clou[illegible]
42½° P.M. [illegible]

At Lincoln is no doubt elected
President of these United States
they say Iowa — I am for [illegible]
I, Alabama from the Union
at all hazzard in the Negro

★

Abram Lincoln
abolitionist
Elected
President

Solely by Northern votes &
with [illegible] hatred to Slavery

7 November 1860

Wednesday November 7th 1860

36½° 5½ A.M. E.W. Thin clou hazy [illegible]
29½° Barometer
47½° E.N. & Raining [illegible]
47½° 9 [illegible] P.M.

South
Carolina
Secedes

failed in its purpose. With Sister Julia and me, our object was to spell words like "ax," "quiz," "vex," words in which the prize letters were used, and if either of us achieved all three in one game it was a cause for celebration, and we added an orange or a slice of cake to our crackers.

I loved to hear Sister Julia tell stories of her girlhood. She was one of a large family, and her father, Mr. William Cooper, indulged his children in every whim. She said that when there were chickens for dinner they would be cooked in various ways to suit each child's taste—roasted, fried, broiled, smothered, and creamed. Everything was freely used and in extravagant abundance—a thread cambic handkerchief was used once and then thrown away. Mr. Cooper made a point of never locking his coal house but said that if anyone wanted coal bad enough to steal it he could have it. He had befriended the Indians on several occasions and had smoked a peace pipe with them. In gratitude to him they had given him the Indian name Ooliska, meaning "double eyes," because he wore glasses.

Mr. Cooper kept a diary and illustrated his entries. Many of these sketches were done with colored crayons and are quite effective. I have in my possession his diary for the year 1860. Concerned with the weather, he always illustrated it at the top of the page. For rain there are long, straight, vertical lines; for fog, tiny dots; for a cloudy day, short, curved strokes close together; for wind, lines radiating from the mouth of a bottle; and for lightning, a red zigzag line across the page. The sun is a circle with surrounding rays. The moon is drawn day by day in its different phases and colored black when it is the dark of the moon. Stars are drawn when particularly bright. Not only the weather but every activity is illustrated. When a condition rather than an object is to be recorded he uses a symbol. Illness is represented by a mortar and pestle or a teapot, which is drawn each day as long as the person is ill. Marriage is indicated by crossed love torches above the names of the contracting parties. Death is indicated by a black coffin resting on two chairs. If the person has been socially prominent, there is drapery above the coffin. If it is a child, there is a small coffin resting on a table. A tombstone and a weeping willow indicate burial. For travel he draws whatever is the means of transportation—horse, carriage, engine, man walking. His own return from a trip is a black "stovepipe" hat. Entries like "Bought 65 chickens today for 15 cts. each" are followed by a group of chickens strutting around; the same for turkeys. "The frogs are vocal tonight" is followed by a row of lily pads with a frog on each. When the first martin is noted, there is one flying across the page. The "first fire of the season" is a grate with a glowing red fire; "the last fire of the season" is an empty grate or a pair of andirons. If he sells any article, a pair of scales is drawn under a large eye (that of Justice). When a slave is purchased, he draws a block with the slave on it and the auctioneer standing by with his hammer. Apropos of a shooting scrape in the community, under the picture of a cadaverous looking man in bed is the inscription: "George Long, the low and dissolute wretch, lies low of gun shot." One entry dated 10 October 1860 runs:

> The Black republicans have carried Pennsylvania upwards of 32 thousand majority. Illinois going same way by 10,000 and Ohio by 25,000
>
> Abe Lincoln's Star culminates
>
> Next comes the contest of the Constitutional South and the unconstitutional North. If the North is not utterly defeated then comes a war of the races.

Mother wanted me to have the advantages of kindergarten, but there was none in our community. Fortunately at this time Miss Jennie Pettit, a kindergarten teacher from Memphis, married and came to Tuscumbia to live. Mother, who had long known and loved her, prevailed upon her to open a kindergarten. She did so and trained two young women in kindergarten technique, with the result that Miss Maud Lindsay and Miss Mary

Sampson opened a kindergarten of their own and Polly Watkins, Miss Maud's niece, and I were their first pupils. Thus it was that Maud Lindsay began her famous career as a kindergarten authority, lecturer, storyteller, and author of children's books.

Travel to
Places Far and Near

LIVING IN A SMALL TOWN, OUR FAMILY DEEMED TRAVEL essential to its way of life, and through the years we traveled much both in this country and abroad.

During my childhood and youth, trains were the important mode of transportation and, as yet, no other has been devised safer or more comfortable, although speed seems now to be the sine qua non.

The railway station was an imposing, if not palatial, building in every city and was not without its importance in small towns. The Southern Railway station in Tuscumbia was famous for many years in this section for its train caller and waitress, Aunt Laura Rutland. She was a heavy-set Negress with a pleasant face, a commanding presence, and an all-embracing manner; she greeted and said farewell to all incoming and outgoing travelers. The ignorant were instructed how to buy tickets and when and where to board the train; babies and luggage received special attention. She knew everybody in town and had a personal greeting for each one who set out on a journey and a hearty welcome for him on his return. On strangers she heaped instructions as to where to stay, how to get there, and what to expect upon getting off the train in the town ahead. A crowded waiting room and platform delighted her. She could then unleash her stentorian voice in calling the train and giving general insturctions. But she was at her best when she knew the incoming train bore a coffin. Then she would sweep through the crowd, arms outstretched, and cry, "Make way, make way for the corpse and the mourners!"

Almost every summer from the time I was four years old Father, Mother, and I spent a month in northern Michigan, where Papá had been going for years. He and Uncle always stayed in Petoskey, and it was there years later that Uncle met Nona Pratt, whom he married. The rest of the family who followed in Papá's train—the Arkansas relatives, Tante, Uncle Weakley, Mother, and Father—spread out into Wequetonsing and Bay View. When I was very young we stayed at Bay View because Mother and Father enjoyed the concerts and lectures—offerings of the Bay View Assembly. There was a kindergarten that I attended. Mother usually chaperoned two or three young ladies, friends who went with us.

We made the trip to Michigan many different ways, but I liked best the journey by boat from Detroit, Cleveland, or Chicago. The first time I remember going was by way of Detroit. We spent the night and part of a day there before taking the boat. I can remember lying awake that night in the hotel listening to the long zum-m-m of the streetcars that grew nearer and nearer until it reached its crescendo, then gradually faded away —a sound that we shall never hear again. To me it was forever after the distinctive city sound. Cleveland stands out predominantly because of its arcade. We arrived late on a Sunday afternoon and to pass the time did window shopping in the arcade that was near our hotel. In one shop I saw the most adorable doll things—little ivory brush and comb sets, powder boxes with puffs, decorated gauze fans with ivory sticks, doll overshoes of real rubber, and Japanese doll tea sets. Mother promised that we would return the next morning and I could make a choice. Back at the hotel, I remember standing at the window looking out over the city and wondering if tomorrow would ever come. Troilus never signed his soul towards the Grecian tents with more longing than I signed mine towards the arcade. In addition to the powder box, fan, and tea set, Mother bought a tweed coat for me while in Cleveland, and I loved it so much that I have never forgotten it.

I enjoyed the boats that carried us for the rest of the trip—the *Northwest* or the *North Land*. Life on boats fascinated me, and still does. At the time of our earliest trips, these boats dropped anchor only in the waters off Mackinac Island; hence we had to be taken ashore in a ferry boat, then by train to Bay View. I remember how delighted we all were when the harbor at Harbor Point was deepened sufficiently for the *North Land* and the *Manitou* to round the point and dock there.

On one trip home when we went to Mackinac Island to take the boat we found that it was going to be very late because

THE *North Land*

it had gone to the rescue of a ship in distress and had taken on board all its passengers, many ill. We were told that the reservations for the group of passengers waiting at Mackinac had been commandeered for the use of those rescued. I can remember the long wait into the night and how the searchlight from the Old Fort on the hill played over the dark waters, adding a feeling of mystery and almost of fear. I recall the shout of joy that went up when it picked out the big white ship in the darkness. After getting on board we were assigned couches in the main salon. Mother put me to bed on one of them and to shield my eyes from the glare of the big chandeliers raised an umbrella over me.

The country around Little Traverse Bay was a paradise for children and still is, with its many charming inland lakes, its beaches and sand dunes, and unsurpassed summer climate. Father, Mother, and I often went earlier than Papá and Uncle. But the Arkansas cousins were always there; for their mother, Aunt Lila, took them up after their return from "Bambam," as they called Alabama, and Uncle Hal joined them later. It was our delight to search the beaches for shells and for agates (which we never found) and for Petoskey rocks, of which we found many—those beautiful and unusual stones with the delicate patterns surrounding each dark spot that, they told us, was once a living creature millions of years ago but was eventually changed into stone. We adored the fishing trips to Round Lake where the fish never failed to bite. Father always took us children on those trips, for he loved to fish. He would hire one of the big flat-bottomed boats and put us all in. Often Mother and the other grownups would come later and join us fishermen for lunch. When all went fishing there were several boatloads.

We children would have two or three hooks on our lines, and at times the water would be so clear that we could see the sun perch and the bluegills when they came up and swallowed the worms on the barbs. Father fished with a different bait and caught larger fish. These would be taken to the boatman's wife in midmorning, and she would prepare them and have them cooked to add to the lunch that our hotel furnished. We spread it in a little clubhouse provided for that purpose.

Always a source of interest were the groups of Indians that, in those days, would come to the hotels to display and sell their beautiful baskets. And we would go on trips to Cross Village, the first settlement in that section and the place where Père Marquette landed and erected a cross in 1672. At the time of our visits it was a community made up almost entirely of Indians. One could watch them making the baskets. From whatever resort we were staying, we would go every few afternoons to Petoskey, either on the dummy or on the ferryboats that made continuous circuits of the bay, stopping at each resort. Of the boats I remember best the *Silver Spray*, the *Searchlight*, and the *America*. To take a moonlight ride on one of these was, I thought, little short of heaven.

A box of chocolates (Allegretti's preferred) and bags of popcorn were standard refreshments for all trips. Everybody one saw had a bag of popcorn, for there were popcorn booths all over the resorts. We children made friends with the men and women inside who did the popping, and they would heap up our bags and pour on an extra amount of melted butter.

Lake Street in Petoskey was lined with fascinating shops of all kinds. But Grant's Auction was our favorite. Our parents or aunts and uncles would be inside, so we had a good excuse to go in; but our real reason was to take a piece, going in and coming out, of Turkish paste from a silver platter heaped with that delectable confection. It was always on a table near the door, and one was supposed to help himself. There were oriental bazaars smelling of incense, with their Syrian proprietors with whom we made friends, especially "Mr. Dick," who was always in a good humor. Little Will's Jewelry Store with its enormous clock that could be seen all along the street kept us time conscious for the treat of the afternoon: no trip to Petoskey was complete without a visit to the Central Drug Store for an ice cream sundae. There was a long counter with covered glass bowls extending its entire length, each one filled with a delicious topping. But which to choose was the problem—chocolate, caramel, coconut, strawberry, cherry, raspberry, et cetera, et cetera. Those were the joyous summers with many of the family there, and we went for so many years that we were sad when we had to leave. The train usually pulled out late in the afternoon—a long line of Pullmans with porters in stiff whitecoats and the dining car all ready with bunches of sweet peas on the tables. As the train slowly moved off I would sit with my face glued to the window watching for familiar haunts, catching the last glimpse of the bay, and gazing over the countryside with its milkweed and goldenrod, its willows and birch trees that I loved, and its tight little houses. I called them "buttoned-up" houses because many of them had a black outside covering with rows of what looked to me like big brass buttons. There were always pots of red geraniums in the windows. The second morning, as we waked up in the hot, humid air of the South, the smell of rank vegetation past its prime would seep into the train, and we would see from the windows piles of watermelons and wagons and mules and many Negroes on the streets. We would know that we were nearing home. Daisy, Ghee's granddaughter who was Uncle's and Nona's maid, returning from her first trip with them to Petoskey, looked out the window and remarked, "Hump, it sho do look low and trashy."

Back home there was always the fun of unpacking the things that we had found on the beach or bought in the shops. The Petoskey rocks were polished to be installed as paperweights, and the baskets and souvenirs bought for gifts were distributed. Then the pretty pieces of china, the Oriental rugs, or the objects of art bought at Grant's Auction were put in place about the house. And there was always a big loaf of maple sugar that we gradually chipped away during the weeks to come.

One summer Father planned a trip to Montana so that Mother could visit her dearest friend, Mrs. Anderson, whom I called Aunt Alma. I was just recovering from a serious illness, and the doctor thought the change would be very beneficial. That trip is still vivid in my memory due, doubtless, to my being extra sensitive to impressions.

I remember the long days on the Pullman as we crossed the great plains and the things the conductor and porter did to entertain me. There were no dining cars then on those transcontinental trains, but stations along the way furnished the meals, and the conductor telegraphed ahead how many passengers to expect. Interested in my gaining some weight, he always asked me what I would like, and if the dish happened to be on the menu he would clap his hands and say it had been ordered for me.

Most of the time I would sit in Father's lap while he talked to me about the country through which we were passing, pointing out the great herds of cattle, "a thousand feeding as one," the groups of Indians in their colorful blankets watching the trains pass, and the cute little gophers sitting so erect by their holes. He pointed out the hillside where Custer and his men were buried, telling me the sad story of Little Big Horn.

Since White Sulphur Springs where Aunt Alma lived was not on the railroad, Mr. Anderson, her husband, met us at the little town of Townsend and drove us the rest of the way in his carriage. I was estatic over the meadows carpeted with beautiful wild flowers and the great trees along the sides of the road. We ate our lunch by a rippling stream under overhanging boughs; the banks were covered with smooth slate-colored rocks. Mother hunted out a flat stone and a pointed one and had me write and draw on them for they were slate.

Aunt Alma had two children about my age—Barclay, six; and Mildred, four. I was five. We had a wonderful time playing together. Her German maid, Libby, was so good to us, always making cookies and buns and taking us places. I had never before seen a Chinaman and so was intrigued by the one who came to the house every morning with great baskets of fresh vegetables suspended from a long pole that he balanced on his shoulders. Libby took us across the meadow to see the Chinaman work his garden and to have him talk to us. His garden was not far from Aunt Alma's house, which was situated near the outskirts of the town with a beautiful view of snow-capped mountains. I was fascinated by the words "snow-capped" and "meadow" and thought them just as beautiful as my favorite "wreath." They appeared frequently in my childish effusions after my return when I secluded myself halfway up the stairway and spent hours composing verses and descriptions of mountains and meadows.

I had my sixth birthday while there. Aunt Alma had a party for me with lots of children invited, a beautiful table, and a birthday cake. While there I went to another little girl's birthday party. We all sat around the table, and the honoree wore a crown of poppies; I was greatly impressed by that. The party was at the home of the Henrys, friends of Aunt Alma, and I learned years later that the little girl was Mrs. Herbert Hoover's youngest sister. I went with Barclay and Mildred to their kindergarten run by Aunt Alma's young friend, Miss Giltnan, to whom I became devoted. When not teaching kindergarten, she lived on a big ranch with her brother. Great was my delight when we were all invited to spend several days at the ranch. There I could ramble over the flower-strewn meadows, and I saw herds of sheep and a real storybook shepherd—an educated man from a foreign country who because of some tragedy in his life wanted to lose himself and took up the life of a shepherd. At that ranch I tasted my first graham crackers. It seems they had just been put on the market and were considered quite a treat. At bedtime they were passed around, and I remember going to bed with my appetite for them completely unsatisfied!

While at the ranch we were taken into the gold mining country where placer mining was being done. I can see now the long flume, the bottom made of round slabs from big trees. At the end of the flume, the gravel washed down was "panned," and I was given a small sample of gold dust, which I kept for many years. One of the miners invited us to have dinner at his cabin. I was told that he was a native of the Azores; that set him and the islands apart in my mind as did the information that he could neither read nor write. I remember the good dinner he had cooked and as we sat down at the table, he jumped up with the exclamation, "My gosh, I've forgotten the rags!"—meaning napkins.

Mother loved to go to Boxwood and visited it frequently as a girl. A trip there in my childhood was always an event. We usually went by train to Trinity, where we were met by a surrey and driven the seven miles to the plantation. In winter the roads were always muddy, and I can remember during the long drive watching the mud stick to the wheels of the surrey, then plop off into the slush as the wheels turned. Sometimes we drove up in our carriage, but that trip would be in the summer and took all day. Courtenay would drive Mother and me, and we would leave early with a lunch that we ate on the banks of Big Nance Creek, where there was a spring and tall cedar trees. I still remember the pungent fragrance of those cedars in the noonday heat and the great stillness of the place, broken only by the chirping of birds.

Boxwood was an old brick house with pointed windows like a Gothic church, and there were two big magnolias in front of the porch, and the yard was a maze of boxwood, some of it so tall Mother could not see over the top—a wonderful place for playing hide-and-seek. There was an old, overgrown garden with big forest trees and festoons of wild grape vines where "swinging in the grape-vine swing" was alluring because precarious. In the garden nearer the house were flowers that kept coming back year after year—zinnias, then called "oldmaids," phlox, verbena, hollyhocks, ragged robins, and larkspur. Long after most of the plantation homes of the South had been deserted by their owners or had been taken over by the tenantry or left to fall into decay, the Elliott descendants continued to live at Boxwood. They were a typical antebellum family, clinging to the old manner of life.

There was Cousin Jerry, Mother's first cousin, a retired physician, his wife, Cousin Fannie, and their two sons, who helped their father run the plantation. In addition there were Cousin Fannie's two sisters, Miss Kate and Miss Jimmy Baker, perfect examples of unmarried Southern gentlewomen—delicate in build, with placid faces, gray hair always in place, voices that had never been raised in anger or in excessive joy, and small hands skilled in needlework. In summer they were immaculate in sprigged muslin, crisp and cool, with ruffles and lace, a brooch at the neckline and a black velvet band around the throat. These two were indispensable members of the household, for it was Miss Kate who kept house and managed the servants. She was the more dignified of the two and always wore a bunch of keys fastened at her belt. Miss Jimmy had a little twinkle in her eye and a merry laugh. She loved children, and you felt that she would have liked to have some fun.

There were many outbuildings on the place and an office in the yard where the boys stayed in summer. And there was a winter and a summer kitchen. The winter kitchen was in the basement where the dining room was located, but the summer kitchen was in one of the outside brick houses like our kitchen. In the basement across the hall from the dining room was the storeroom, which, always under lock and key, seemed a kind of holy of holies, particularly as it had a swinging shelf loaded with all manner of good things—chocolate cake, coconut cake, muffin cakes, tea cakes, pickles, preserves, jellies, custards, and pies. Because it was hanging from the ceiling and held all of these delights, that shelf became associated in my mind with the hanging gardens of Babylon. If possible, I followed Miss Kate when she went downstairs to the basement and into the storeroom, for she always gave me a muffin cake or, sometimes, a slice of one of the layer cakes.

Other relatives lived on another part of the plantation, and their home was called Rose Hill; in its heyday the Elliott plantation was one of the largest and finest in the Tennessee Valley.

There were young children at Rose Hill and also the Lile and Moseley children and other connections in Trinity; when Mother and I arrived for a visit, the children that were my age were sent to play with me. They would come not only in the day but sometimes would spend the night. Cousin Jerry and his boys would play games with us—blind man's bluff and hide-and-seek, which would send us racing all over the big house, hiding in wardrobes, under stairways and beds. "Miss Kitsy" was another game that provoked much laughter. Cousin Jerry would disappear and with Miss Kate's help would dress up and return as a lady eight feet tall. One of the boys, acting as stage manager, would introduce her to us as "Miss Kitsy" and would give her orders and put her through her stunts to our squeals of delight. If Miss Kate disappeared again we knew it was a good sign that she would be back shortly with plates of cake, which we would eat in front of the big wood fire in the library. How well I remember that room.

OLD SYNODICAL COLLEGE

Over the mantel was an engraving of Landseer's "Dignity and Impudence"; on either end of the mantel were tall glass globes that covered a boy and girl, each standing under a rose tree in full bloom. There were shells with painted scenes inside that had been brought from Florida, and a round center table with a green baize cover that hung low, edged with ball fringe. A lamp and books rested on it, and Cousin Jerry had a special chair under the window by the fireplace.

During the day we children played under the old magnolia trees, making hats with long streamers and capes out of the magnolia leaves, which we pinned together with little twigs and decorated with the flowers we were allowed to pull in the garden. Or we would play hide-and-seek in the boxwood maze, or holler down the rainbarrel at the corner of the back porch and listen for the echo, or swing in the grape vines, or go roaming over the place, or fishing in nearby Fox's Creek, or riding horseback down soft country lanes.

Once Mother was sent for when Cousin Jerry was critically ill. I was too young then for her to leave; so she took me with her. Cousin Fannie was deeply religious and as I later realized was in no way reticent in expressing either her beliefs or demands upon others. The family was all assembled, and when we arrived I was sent upstairs to the room to which the children had been assigned. I can remember how uncomfortable I felt and with what dread I toiled up the steps when I heard that they had all been sent up there to pray. I felt that I was in for deep mortification, for I did not know how to pray except to say "Now I lay me down to sleep," and it was not night and I was not going to bed. Fortunately for me, no mention of prayer was made among the children after my arrival, but we amused ourselves by poking the logs in the fireplace and as sparks flew upward exclaiming, "Don't you wish you had that many dollars?" I heard Mother tell afterwards that the children had sent word to Cousin Fannie to let them stop praying and trust a while.

My father in the course of his practice of law would, at

intervals, have to go to a small town, the county seat of a neighboring county—a place most inaccessible from where we lived. To get there for the opening of court, he had to leave at four o'clock in the morning on a freight train, get off at the nearest town, and be driven the rest of the way in a buggy over almost impassable roads. The night before such a journey, a tray would be carried upstairs with the necessary things for Mother to boil an egg and make him a cup of tea (my mother and father drank tea instead of coffee) on the grate fire and make toast on a toasting fork before he left. Such doings fascinated me, and I longed to go with him. I wanted to have breakfast cooked on a grate where you used a trivet and a little black iron stew pan and to eat it while it was yet night and to ride on a caboose with a man swinging a red lantern. I wanted to see the old hotel about which I had heard so many stories—how the lawyers had to cut corn cobs out of its mattresses before they could go to sleep and sometimes found it more comfortable to sleep in chairs, as Father did. And I wanted to see its famous cake and its brass spoons.

One summer when Father was going and returning the same day, he said that I could go with him. The early morning breakfast and leave taking were exciting, and I left with great anticipation. Mother had fixed a little lunch for me because she thought I should not eat the food at the hotel. To have fixed one for Father would have meant no more cases in that county, as he would tell her when she suggested his taking a silver spoon to use instead of the brass one. The ride in the caboose was disappointing; it was so uncomfortable. But the thought of what was in store sustained me.

The rough drive in the surrey finally brought us to the town, with its courthouse square in which stood giant oak trees. Across the street was the hotel, a dun-colored, one story house, ell-shaped with a porch filling up the space made by the ell. I had eaten my lunch before we arrived; I don't remember what I did until the old proprietor, who was bent in the shape of a scythe, rang the big bell, and the lawyers all filed into the dining room and took seats around a long oval table. There in the center of the table was the famous cake, the very one a venturesome young lawyer had attempted to slice only to find it was a cheese hoop that had been iced.

When all were seated, the bent old man and his equally bent sisters marched around the table poking a platter at each guest and in turn calling out, "Goat? Goat? Goat? Pig? Pig? Pig? Bread? Bread? Bread?" while a slatternly Negro followed pouring coffee into the cups, by each of which lay a brass spoon.

We had to return as we came, but as it happened the freight train was throwing off crossties at short intervals along the track and so getting later and later as it crawled homeward. I can remember how hard the bench was along the side of the caboose where we had to sit, how the moonlight fell through the opened door onto the bare, unkept floor. I can still hear the thud of the crossties as they were thrown off and feel the desperation with which I announced to my father, "If we don't get home in another half hour, I'm going to begin to kick!" He must have thought my threat justified, for I do not remember that he forbade my doing so.

Unusual Guests
and Interesting Characters

GHEE ALWAYS SPOKE OF GUESTS "PRESIDING" IN THE HOUSE. Her choice of words was better than she knew, for there were some who did *preside*. Southern hospitality has the wishes of the guest always prevailing; some guests took advantage of this generosity—whether consciously or unconsciously, I know not.

There was the schoolmate of Father's, unheard of for thirty years, who wrote that she and her little girl would be in Tuscumbia on a certain day and would like to call in the evening. Mother wrote her at once and invited the two of them for dinner. They accepted the invitation. After dinner they stayed and stayed. As twelve o'clock approached Mother invited them to spend the night. They declined as they said they were leaving on the three a.m. train, but they continued to stay on. Yielding at last to Mother's gentle persuasion, the lady consented to her little girl's lying down and later lay down herself (to my great regret I had been put to bed). Since the day of cars and taxis had not arrived, Father had to hitch up the horse and phaeton and take them to the train at that unearthly hour.

To me the supreme test of Mother's hospitality was in connection with a relative who came to convalesce after an operation and had her meals served in whatever room in the house she happened to be, and she made the rounds, porch included. When she left, she joined her son arriving on a train from a nearby city. Among the farewell pleasantries Mother said to the son, "It's too bad you couldn't have spent the weekend with us." Regrets were expressed, the whistle blew, "All aboard" was sounded, hands waved, and the train pulled out. Wearily Mother and I got in the car and rode home, for we had had a trying month. Soon after we settled into the house, the telephone rang. I heard Mother cry in a somewhat anxious tone, "Where are you?" Then came the gay, cheerful response, "Of course, we will be delighted to have you back. I will send for you at once." In the two miles that separated Tuscumbia from Sheffield, mother and son, having discussed the invitation, decided to accept it, got off the train, and telephoned their decision. Not by word or tone of voice during that long weekend did Mother show anything but pleasure in having them. I fear I did not completely follow her example.

Once a distant cousin by marriage, whom none of us had ever seen, wrote Papá that she wanted to come for a visit. He and Mother extended an invitation immediately. The moment she arrived she announced the purpose of her visit, "I am getting even," she said. "All my life I have entertained relatives and friends, have kept open house with never a vacation. Now that my children are grown, I have decided to make a tour visiting all of my kin people and friends. It is true that none of you have ever visited me, but that doesn't matter. I am getting even all the same." Mother must have wondered when her own turn would come.

Cousin Lou also arrived suddenly. She, too, was unknown to us. She was traveling on some church mission. We vividly remember her conversation, which was without pause, and her telescope, a kind of luggage favored at that time for its carrying capacity. She was scheduled to leave on that dreadful three a.m. train. Uncle was delegated to take her to the station. Hearing that she had only one piece of luggage and seeing that she was young and buxom, he suggested that they walk the not too many blocks to the station (he hated to hitch up the horse and phaeton), but he became fearful when he saw as they started that the upper half of the telescope instead of fitting down over the lower half barely overlapped it and that the heavily packed halves were held together by two worn leather straps. About halfway to the station they broke!

There was the steady stream of summer relatives and all-through-the-year irregulars. One cousin among these was a sweet, gentle woman but strong-willed—to quote Ghee's characterization, "soft but terminated-like"—and a person of great religious fervor. Her conversation was almost exclusively on religious subjects. I can remember my tongue-tied embarrassment when she took me to her room, had me kneel down by a chair, and told me to pray and how thankful I should be for all my blessings. She and Mother would have long religious conversations; overhearing fragments of them, Courtenay and Uncle composed a dialogue therefrom and when she left recited it to the family.

In many Southern families, ours among them, giving up one's room to a guest was another of the unwritten laws of hospitality. When I was graduated to an upstairs room (first I had the little room downstairs opening off Mother's), I became a victim. Whenever guests were imminent, Mother would say, "I think you had better let them have your room; it's so much more comfortable. You can stay in one of the guest rooms." After many moves back and forth across the hall—the front upstairs rooms were identical in size, shape, and fenestration—I rebelled in what I thought was a rather adroit manner. When there was a lull in the flow of guests, I asked Mother if I might permanently change my room to the guest room across the hall. "Why, of course," she said. "You can have any room you want." Before the arrival of the next guest Mother made the usual request. "But Mother," I explained, "the room I just moved out of you have always said was the most comfortable." She saw the ruse and laughed heartily. Never again did I have to give up my room.

In our neighborhood lived Miss Puss Cooley and her brother, William, both stone deaf. There had been another sister, Miss Bird, but she had died before I knew the family. Their house fascinated me. It was tall and gaunt, a two story brick

Cabin with Fence   Mary Wallace Kirk

CABIN WITH FENCE

home, and in the late afternoon I could see the sun shining through its curtainless upstairs windows turning them into squares of gold. Sometimes I watched the swallows that swirled about the chimneys and counted those that darted in after each circling flight. I first went to the Cooley home with my mother, who was taking Miss Puss magazines and fruit. Mother wanted me to see the scenic wallpaper in the house, which had been brought from Europe long before by Miss Puss's uncle, an old sea captain. In one room, I remember, there was a foxhunt with pink-coated horsemen set in a brilliant landscape, but faded in glory. The paper hung in strips and swayed gently in any breeze.

We had to pound on the door with rocks to announce our arrival. Miss Puss finally admitted us, delighted to have company. She began at once in her high shrill voice to relate the doings of the neighborhood, calling by names every guest we had had during the summer. Yet she had never left home! A great reader and a poor sleeper, she told Mother that her brother complained greatly at her extravagance in burning a lamp all night. "I tell him," she said, "I can't hear, but I will *see!*" But her great passion in life was snuff. She confided to Mother that if her finances were ever reduced to a dime (and they were fast slipping to that) and she had no bread and no snuff she would spend the dime for snuff. And when William again complained, she rebuked him, "What better are you? You don't do anything but chew tobacco!" These two chewed and dipped away their lives. The house fell in over their heads until only one room was habitable, and there Miss Puss died.

Miss Julia was a little old lady with fluttering eyelashes. When she walked, she hopped like a bird, and she caught her breath between her words, so that she almost seemed to hop when she talked. I thought it a great treat to be allowed either going or coming from town to stop at her house and the store next door kept by her and her brother, for they sold the most delectable little white candy pigs with red peppermint eyes and marshmallow and chocolate brooms with pencils for handles.

But the greatest delight was the little glass houses hung with prisms that sat on tables in Miss Julia's parlor. They were filled with bouquets of flowers—roses, peonies, dahlias, some made of colored wool and some of colored feathers. In the place of honor was a fringe tree (a "grandsire graybeard" the mountain people call it). It was made of fringed white domestic and stood in a tall glass case also hung with prisms. Preserved in alcohol was a large night-blooming cereus. And written on the apothecary jar that held it was the date on which it had been picked and the subsequent date of every addition of alcohol. From either side of the mantel hung baskets with saucers used as bottoms. These baskets were made of gaily colored beads and finished with long tassles. On the mantel were wreaths and crosses and anchors made of the pith of the cochorus plant.

When she told me that she had one time made doll furniture from some of this pith, I spent many days of my childhood looking for a cochorus bush that I never found. Large balls of colored wool rolled around the floor, playthings for her cat.

Miss Julia had had a sad love affair. After she and her fiancé had come home from church one Sunday evening, he had smoked a cigar in her presence. Although they were sitting in the garden, the aroma of the cigar reached her father. Because no gentleman ever smoked in the presence of a lady, he ordered him off the place and commanded his daughter never to see her lover again. And she never did. She consoled herself by making feather flowers.

One day our minister brought a lady to see Mother; I remember her because she looked different from anyone I had ever seen before. She seemed to be dressed like a man, no trousers, of course, but a dark coat like a man's with a long skirt that came to the floor; and she wore a stiff and narrow white bow at her throat. I think she and the minister must have come soliciting funds. I was told later that she was Miss Amelia Brewer, a distinguished lady, and sister of Justice Brewer of the Supreme Court of the United States. Anything that had to do with lawyers or courts I always remembered. She lived way out in the mountains, had a school there, and taught the poor mountain children.

Somehow the memory of her and her strangeness stayed with me. When I grew up and drove with Father out into the mountains and the remote sections of the county where she had taught, Father introduced me to old men in the country stores who might have known her. From those who had, I learned of her.

Miss Brewer was a deeply religious woman who had been a Congregational missionary at Cape Town, Africa, for seven years before she came to the little community of Alsoboro, Alabama, to teach white and colored children together. She was not only a sister of Justice Brewer, but a niece of Cyrus W. Field. A college was to have been built for her at Alsoboro, but when the people stipulated that it should be "for whites only" she refused to have it built. Then she was run out of the community. Undaunted, she moved further into the mountains to what the old men called "flat woods" and there taught both day school and Sunday school in the church. She then built her own school and lived above it. Public funds were granted for a three-month session, but she taught nine months, furnishing books and clothing for the pupils from boxes sent to her from the East. Later she built a house for herself and had girls board with her and go to school. She visited everybody and "gave moral instruction wherever she went." Some of the people loved her; some hated her. One old man who had been her pupil said, "She was a mighty smart woman, but when people shouted in church, it scared her, and she told them it would scare the Lord too."

There was a family we knew who lived some distance back in the mountains. In the early days they had made the mistake of settling on the mountain instead of in the valley. They were people of some education and refinement with a love of books that they had passed on to their children, who cherished an old copy of Cowper's poems. But when the men died the old mother and two daughters were left with little in the way of a livelihood. One of them, who had been married, had a daughter and a son. They lived on what they raised in their garden plot, needlework, and the sale of wild fruits—blackberries, plums, huckleberries, and muscadines—as they came in season. Often they had for sale little bundles of "fat" pine. I first remember them walking in three or four miles from the mountain with these commodities for sale. Mother always bought what they had and usually gave them a box of canned goods to take home. She gave them an old baby buggy, the kind with a long body that could be used as a push cart; and she always had the unmarried sister hem her linen napkins and also gave her zephyr to crochet baby saques and caps. I think Mother had one set made for every baby she knew. She crocheted a saque and cap for my doll just out of appreciation. They loved to read, and Mother gave them magazines and loaned them books. The married sister, a kind of religious exhorter, felt called upon to give religious and moral instruction to the mountain people. Nathan-like, she would not hesitate to say "Thou art the man" when she thought necessary. She once told Mother of her longing for a self-pronouncing Bible; Mother ordered one for her.

In time they acquired an ox and cart, and they came into town more frequently with their wares. The young daughter longed for broader horizons and went to Nashville, Tennessee, and secured a job in a snuff factory. But she fell ill and returned home and was an invalid for many years. She had a passion for books, and Mother kept her supplied. Every few weeks her brother came by in the oxcart and carried her eight or ten. She took beautiful care of them and always returned them. It was at that time that she began writing verses. She got well and brought them in for Mother to read and to help her get them published. Mother sent the best poem in the lot to the *Christian Observer* and asked them to publish it, which they did. One Sunday afternoon Father, Mother, and I took the paper with the poem in it to her. We could not get up to the house on account of the lack of a road, but she saw the car and came out. As she stood reading her poem, the blood began slowly to mount from neck to throat to cheeks until it suffused her entire face and head. When she had finished, her only comment was, "I see they haven't made any typographical errors." She began to bring Mother bunches of wild azaleas, crab apples, and other flowering shrubs. Once when handing Mother a bunch of mountain laurel she said, "I went to the edge of the cliff this morning and looked over and behold, and lo, the laurel was in bloom!"

Mother

MY MOTHER WAS THE MOST CHARMING PERSON I HAVE EVER known and the most fun to be with. She enlivened and ennobled all that she touched, and her conversation was always fresh and sparkling because watered by a clear stream bubbling up from the recesses of a beautifully cultivated mind.

Buoyant by nature, she did not hesitate to admit happiness, to express affection for people and places and things. Although a sufferer from arthritis for many years and in constant pain, she never gave up but always, to use her phrase, "kept the faculty of effort alive." When the disease cruelly confined her, I, after leaving her alone for some hours, would ask, "What have you been doing?" "Just making love to the house" would be her joyous reply. Lavish in praise, she often quoted in justification Benjamin West's response to his mother's rapturous kiss when he showed her his first drawing—"That kiss made me a painter." She was equally responsive to joy or sorrow, passing from one emotion to another with what to me as a child seemed incredible ease. Ghee often said, "If I would cry as easy as Miss Ella I think I could get religion."

She found people unfailingly interesting, amusing, and lovable. An inimitable mimic and raconteur, she could impersonate anyone with rare felicity. Father, a very considerate person, once said to her, "My Dear, aren't you afraid people will think you are making fun of them?" "No, I have never made fun of anyone; I only see the fun they make."

ELLA RATHER KIRK

She never lost the spirit of youth; at high noon and in later years she kept the freshness of her morning. When she was over eighty and dressed for a party, she would say to me, "If they put me with the old ladies, *please* rescue me." In a sense she was a timid person, never pushing herself or ever accepting opportunities that her talents merited or would have adorned. It was in her own home among loved and familiar surroundings that she fully blossomed:

> Here was her golden prime
> And still the haunt beloved a virtue yields.

She gave generously of herself—"the true aristocrat who preferred to give rather than to take." She was a great favorite of the Arkansas boys, who came for a month over many summers. One of them after he was grown wrote to her every week up to the time of her death, and she welcomed his letters with all the eagerness of a girl. "I loved her with all my heart," he told me.

Mother did not like the routine of housekeeping, but with a swift touch she got chores done and the way cleared for enjoyment. Once a new maid said to her, "Mrs. Kirk, you turns around so fast you scares me." Our house was a place where guests loved to come. Many came over the years, and Mother loved to have it so. She would hold out her arms to them in the most heart-warming welcome. She was known for her hospitality and good food and a delightful sense of humor.

Our house had always been the place where visiting ministers were entertained. Once when the Methodist Conference met here, Mother offered to take in four of the delegates. They were interesting men whom the whole family enjoyed. Papá became a great favorite with them, and they had a group picture made with him in the center and called it *The Bishop and his Cabinet*. The last day of their stay the cook failed to come, but Mother did not let them even suspect. That night in telling Father how she had managed she recounted the leave-taking of the last minister, "He handed me a dollar and said, 'Will you please give this to the cook; she has been so kind.' 'Thank you,' I said, 'I'm the cook.' 'My dear, you did not say that, did you?' 'Of course not!' "

I remember the lovely bunches of flowers that came from her greenhouse. Mother loved to work with flowers; she always had pots of hyacinths, oxalis, or primroses, bowls of white narcissi, and window boxes of delicate white Roman hyacinths. All of these she brought into the house in winter. She put a window box of crocuses in my little room. She would arrange bouquets of heliotrope, freesias, lemon verbena, pink geraniums, purple and white Parma violets and send them to sick friends with a gay note or a bit of original doggerel. In summer she spent much time in the garden where we often had meals. She would bring in sprays of ambrosia and lemon verbena to put between the fresh sheets when they were put away after having been laundered. Among her friends there was always a coterie of little girls. She would tell them stories, give them luncheons, and, as they grew older, lend them books, which she discussed with them.

Mother was a great letter writer. She wrote as she talked and dashed off letters as she waited for the family to assemble for breakfast or at odd moments in a busy day. During my four years at college I had a daily letter from her, so I never lost touch with the family's doings. The most trivial detail glowed beneath her touch. The arrival of her letters was occasion for a family gathering in the household where they were received. Her friendships were lifelong. One friend she corresponded with for sixty-five years with no diminution of delight though they were a continent apart for most of the time. Whatever she did, she did rapidly. A photographic reader, she read widely, sometimes a book a day.

She was of an earlier, fairer time that bred the subtle aura of personality that we call distinction. She found life good, the mere living of it, and I have heard her say that she would gladly relive it. To her way of thinking "those who loudly proclaim

their disenchantment with life have never been enchanted by it."
After her death a friend wrote:

> I will always think of Mrs. Kirk as she appeared that
> lovely winter afternoon when it was my pleasure to meet
> her. So much a part she seemed of that rich and beautiful
> room. She was sitting at the end of the long sofa, near the
> fire, a wonderful figure out of a past time that was mak-
> ing its mark on the present.

Envoy

THROUGH THE OPEN WINDOW HERE IN THE LIBRARY I SEE the lush, watermelon pink blossoms of myrtles and the crisp althea blooms with crimson throats glistening in the morning sunlight. These old-fashioned flowers have always been a part of my life, and it is one of the joys of summer to greet their return. I connect them with the recollections and scenes of my childhood that during the past months have flashed on my inward eye like pictures on a screen. Now that the last picture has been shown, I am conscious of how the pressures of modernity have effected some changes in the conduct of life at Locust Hill. But certainly its tradition of hospitality remains. Guests still arrive, invited or self-invited, singly or in groups, in winter and in summer, in spring and in autumn. Whether they are the youngest little Rathers, who belong to the sixth generation, or Tante, who boasts a hundred years; whether they come from overseas, as many have, or from my homeland—all are welcomed.

Hospitality at Locust Hill today would not be possible without the help of my good friends Mable Mullins and Jack Woods, Elmore and Kate Steele, and William Owes and Henry Moorman, who have taken Isaiah's place in the garden. A priceless possession is their kindness and their loyalty throughout the years, those before and those since I have been at Locust Hill alone.

In writing of everyday ways of life at Locust Hill, I have

MARY WALLACE KIRK

surveyed a hundred years of varied living here—especially the warm contentment of the years of my childhood:

> So I remember each new morning
> From childhood
> . . .
> Of a sun-drenched world, a lake
> Of light through which light falls,
> . . .
> The world is a circle where all move
> Before after, after before,
> And my aware awaking loves
> The day.
> STEPHEN SPENDER, "Awakening"

MARY WALLACE KIRK AND SIX OF HER BOY COUSINS

THE GROUNDS FROM THE GATHERING PLACE ON THE PORCH

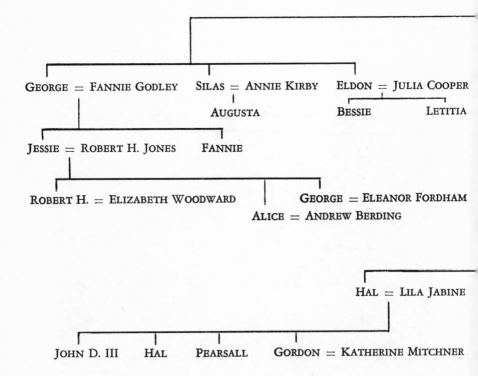

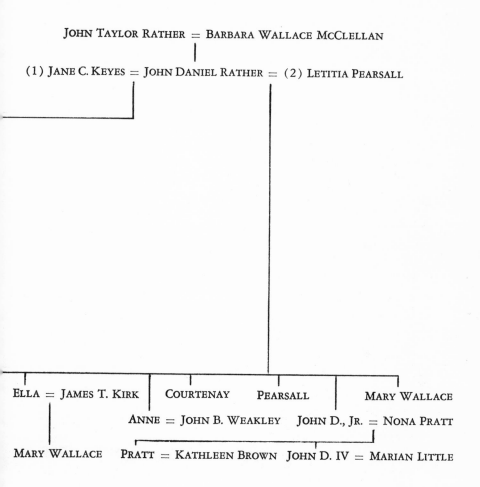

R. F. D.   Mary Wallace Kirk